Contents

Infertility Matters in Healthcare

Julian Jenkins

Liz Corrigan

and

Ruth Chambers

RADCLIFFE MEDICAL PRESS

Radcliffe Medical Press Ltd
18 Marcham Road
Abingdon
Oxon OX14 1AA
United Kingdom

www.radcliffe-oxford.com
The Radcliffe Medical Press electronic catalogue and online ordering facility.
Direct sales to anywhere in the world.

———————————————————

British Library Cataloguing in Publication Data

A catalogue record for this book is available from the British Library.

ISBN 1 85775 960 5

Typeset by Joshua Associates Ltd, Oxford
Printed and bound by TJ International Ltd, Padstow, Cornwall

Preface

Patients want simple, clear information about the options, risks and implications of infertility treatment when they are feeling emotional at a vulnerable stage of their lives. They often ask their doctors for explanations and advice about their feelings and experiences of treatment. GPs and hospital doctors in turn need clear unambiguous information about best practice in a complex field, to be able to explain and discuss the complicated medical management and ethical dilemmas that face their patients who are seeking assistance for their infertility.

It is difficult for patients and doctors to keep abreast of all the new and complex developments in fertility treatment. Patients need to understand and think through the issues to be able to fully participate in the decisions made about their care.

It is really important for the welfare of the child-to-be and the would-be parents, that GPs work closely with fertility experts to provide seamless care for infertile couples. Some GPs shy away from the seeming complexities of fertility treatments and are reluctant to contribute to the assessment of couples' suitability as prospective parents. Clear and specific information should enable health professionals and patients alike to understand the complicated medical and ethical situations that are integral to the management of those with infertility and participate more fully in decisions about their care.

This book seeks to describe current thinking and best practice in the management of infertility in such a way that those doctors, other health professionals or patients who are new to the field can appreciate the key issues and concerns. It draws heavily on the publications from the Human Fertilisation and Embryology Authority and the evidence-based clinical guidelines on the management of infertility published by the Royal College of Obstetricians and Gynaecologists, which were supported by the clinical effectiveness programme of the NHS Executive.

Guidelines are raining down on GPs' heads from all directions, some offering conflicting advice, others complicated instructions. The Royal College of Obstetricians and Gynaecologists' guidelines[1,2] give the evidence for best practice in managing infertility in primary and specialist care settings. They have been developed by a multidisciplinary group including GPs, nurses and users, as well as fertility experts, overseeing a dedicated research team undertaking systematic reviews of the literature on the topic. The draft guidelines were peer reviewed by a variety of health professionals and patients, and amended accordingly. The resulting national guidelines are intended to be adapted to local circumstances and used for commissioning high quality infertility care. For simplicity the main guidelines, reviews and reports will be referred to in support of the information given here, rather than the references being given to the hundreds of individual published research papers that they considered. The guidelines[1,2] themselves are graded according to how robust the evidence cited is, and whether statements are scientifically proven, are backed by good research or are the opinion of experts in the field.

We know that GPs who use infertility guidelines are more likely to undertake a more comprehensive work-up prior to referral, including seeing and examining both partners, initiating basic investigations and speeding up the referral process.[3]

Julian Jenkins
Liz Corrigan
Ruth Chambers
January 2003

References

1 Royal College of Obstetricians and Gynaecologists (1998) *The initial investigation and management of the infertile couple. Evidence-based clinical guidelines. No. 2.* Royal College of Obstetricians and Gynaecologists, London.
2 Royal College of Obstetricians and Gynaecologists (1998) *The management of infertility in secondary care. Evidence-based clinical guidelines. No. 3.* Royal College of Obstetricians and Gynaecologists, London.
3 Emslie C, Grimshaw J and Templeton A (1993) Do clinical guidelines improve general practice management and referral of infertile couples? *BMJ.* **306**: 1728–31.

About the authors

Julian Jenkins has extensive experience in the field of infertility and a particular interest in the application of information technology to education, clinical practice and research. He is the Clinical Director of the Centre for Reproductive Medicine, University of Bristol, (www.ReproMED.co.uk). He is the Chairman of the website editorial board and a member of the Executive Committee of the British Fertility Society (www.britishfertilitysociety.org.uk). He is the Chairman of a taskforce developing a classification system for infertility for the European Society for Human Reproduction and Embryology (www.ecit.info), a member of the American Society for Reproductive Medicine and the Menstrual Disorder, and the Infertility Panel of the Cochrane Collaboration. He is the Associate Medical Director for IM&T at the United Bristol Healthcare Trust (www.ubht.org.uk), the Course Director of an MSc course in Reproduction & Development (www.ReD-MSc.org.uk), the Chairman of the Obstetrics & Gynaecology Education Committee for the South West Region (www.swot.org.uk), a member of the international editorial board of Ferti.net (www.ferti.net) and a member of both the Royal College of Obstetricians & Gynaecologists Guidelines & Audit Committee, and the Information Services Committee (www.rcog.org.uk).

Liz Corrigan has been actively involved in infertility treatment since 1980. In 1985, she joined the University of Bristol, Centre for Reproductive Medicine, where she is currently the Business Manager and Nursing Director. In addition to her SRN she gained an MBA with Oxford Brookes University and a BA(Hons) Degree with the Open University. In order to improve clinical care she combines treatment with research. Her main interests are infertility management, including assisted conception particularly considering the quality of care, and issues relating to outcome of treatment. Since 1996 she has been an inspector for the Human Fertilisation and Embryology Authority (HFEA). Despite her increasing managerial involvement, she keeps in close touch with patients and both local and national support groups. Her international contribution to infertility practice was recognised when she was recently made the Chairman of the European Society of Human Reproduction & Embryology Paramedical Group.

Ruth Chambers has been a GP for more than 20 years and is currently the Professor of Primary Care Development at Staffordshire University. She was a member of the HFEA in the late 1990s. Ruth has designed and organised many types of educational initiatives, including distance-learning programmes. Recently, she has developed a keen interest in working with GPs, nurses and others in primary care around clinical governance and practice personal and professional development plans. This book is one of a series that she has co-authored with experts in various fields that integrate personal development with learning that is targeted at service delivery.

Acknowledgements

We are very grateful to colleagues from the Human Fertilisation and Embryology Authority (HFEA) for their detailed feedback on the first edition of the book as it was compiled. Much of the material in the book has been informed by the extensive working papers and documents produced by the HFEA which anticipate and address medical and ethical issues arising from assisted reproduction. We should also like to acknowledge the contribution that the *Guidelines* on the management of infertility published by the Royal College of Obstetricians and Gynaecologists have made to this book and will make to those working in primary care and hospital settings.

The material about clinical governance (in Chapter 1) and personal development planning (in Chapter 10) is based on the original work of Drs Gill Wakley and Ruth Chambers.

Part One:
Learning about infertility

Introduction

The material in this book sets out how learning more about the management of fertility problems and reviewing current practice can be incorporated into your personal development plan. You need to develop a dual focus on improving the clinical management of patients with infertility problems and increasing the efficiency of the working environment in your organisation. Team members should work together to direct their individual learning plans to form their workplace personal and professional development plan. The additional workload for NHS staff pursing best practice, and undertaking collaborative working and training, has resource implications, so your learning plans should complement the business plan of the general practice or hospital trust where you work.

If as a GP, community nurse or junior doctor working on a gynaecology unit, infertility practice is not the sole focus of your work, you may decide to allocate 50% of your annual personal development plan to infertility matters. On the other hand, if you work in a fertility unit you may want to focus your learning plan exclusively on infertility practice – although you could combine clinical topics with honing personal skills in time management or communication. Your learning plan should be shaped by whatever topics are important for you, your workplace or practice team and your patient population. Your plan will be based on the preliminary work you undertake to clarify and prioritise what you need to learn, or how you make improvements to your services.

We have included extracts from a patient's story throughout the book describing the course of her own infertility and experience of treatments and investigations. Seeing things from the patient's perspective should bring home to you what an emotional toll fertility treatment takes.

The first chapter of the book describes how a clinical governance culture incorporates effective clinical management and well-organised working conditions. You should be able to demonstrate that you are fit to practise as an individual clinician or manager (best practice in the management of infertility problems in this case); and that your working environment is fit to practise from. This section should help you to understand more of the context within which you work and how your individual contribution fits into the whole picture of healthcare.

Thereafter each chapter gradually builds up your knowledge base of infertility practice, so that you can bring yourself up to date with the most recent evidence for managing fertility problems. There have been a great many changes in recommended best practice in the past few years. In most cases we cite evidence from a review or compendium rather than the original literature, to simplify the text in this book.

The whole programme builds up to the composing of a personal development plan in Chapter 10. We give four worked examples – these should be appropriate for a GP or nurse working in a general practice setting and an infertility specialist nurse or infertility consultant working in a hospital setting. Interactive exercises at the end of each chapter give readers an opportunity to assess their learning needs, review their performance or that of the team or organisation, and reflect on what improvements to make.

You should transfer information from these needs assessment exercises to the relevant slots in your personal development plan.[1] Adopt a wide-based approach to improving quality – think of how you are establishing a clinical governance culture in your own practice or trust team through your timed action plans.[2]

Resources to support this book are provided on the ReproMED website at www.ReproMED.org.uk/book/.

What should you do next?

Study the template for a personal development plan on pages 122 to 129. You will be filling this in as you complete the reflection exercises or work through the book and continue with your own self-directed learning.

Make changes as a result – to your workplace, to your services, to the advice or information you give to patients, or the way you manage and investigate infertility or complicating problems.

References

1 Wakley G, Chambers R and Field S (2000) *Continuing Professional Development in Primary Care: making it happen.* Radcliffe Medical Press, Oxford.

2 Chambers R and Wakley G (2000) *Making Clinical Governance Work for You.* Radcliffe Medical Press, Oxford.

CHAPTER 1

Clinical governance and infertility practice

Clinical governance is about doing anything and everything required to maximise the quality of healthcare or services, including for those with fertility problems.[1]

The Commission for Health Improvement (CHI) defines clinical governance as: 'the framework through which NHS organisations and their staff are accountable for the quality of patient care' including:

- a patient-centred approach
- up-to-date clinical care
- high standards and safety
- improvement in patient services and care.[2]

Clinical governance is inclusive – making quality everyone's business, whether they are a doctor, a nurse or other health professional, a manager, a member of staff or a strategic planner. Good infertility practice relies on the multidisciplinary team to support the patient or couple with infertility problems. Delivering best practice requires sufficient clinical staff who are up-to-date and relate well to their patients, and efficient systems and procedures that are patient friendly.

Components of clinical governance

The components of clinical governance are not new. Bringing them together under the banner of clinical governance and introducing more explicit accountability for performance is a new style of working.

The following 14 themes are core components of professional service development, which together form a comprehensive approach to providing high quality healthcare services and clinical governance.[1] These are illustrated in Figure 1.1.

If you interweave these 14 components into your individual and

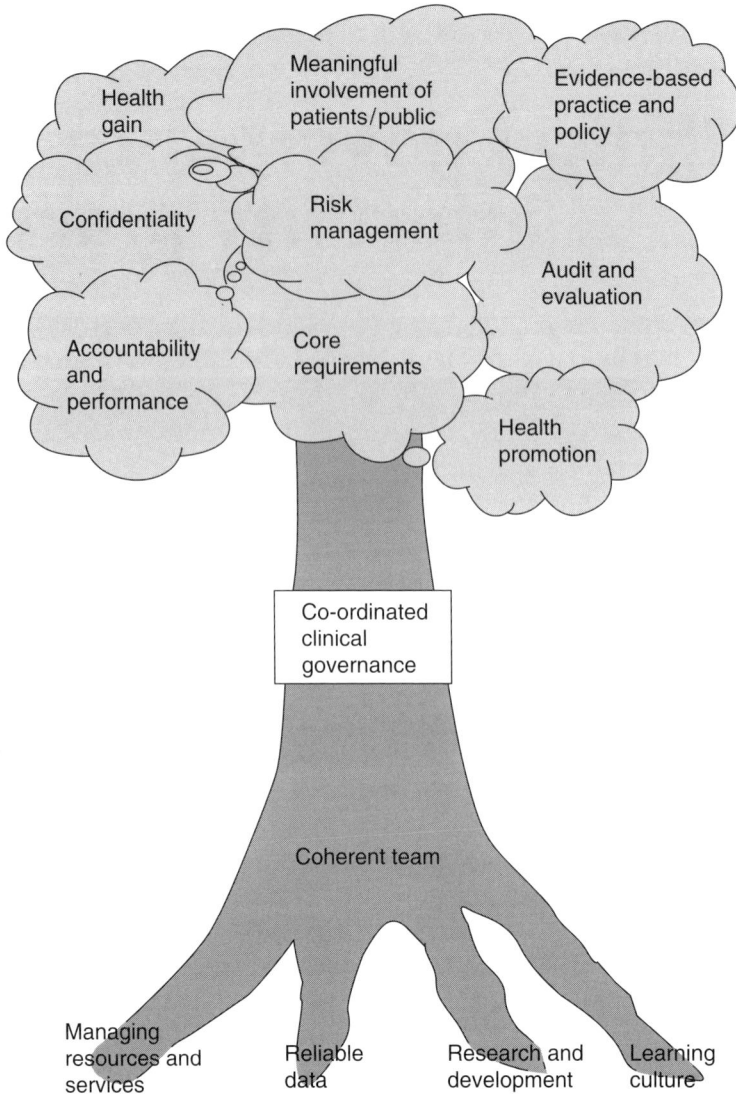

Figure 1.1: 'Routes' and branches of clinical governance.

practice learning plans you will have addressed the requirements for clinical governance at the same time.[1,3]

- Learning culture: for patients and staff in the practice or primary care organisation or within the hospital trust in secondary care.
- Research and development culture: in the workplace or throughout the health service.

- Reliable and accurate data: in the practice, across the primary care organisation or hospital trust and the NHS as a seamless whole.
- Well-managed resources and services, as individuals, as a workplace, across the NHS and in conjunction with other organisations.
- Co-ordinated teamworking: well-integrated teams, including staff working in different healthcare settings.
- Meaningful involvement of patients and the public: including those with infertility problems, those who provide healthcare for them and the general population.
- Health gain: from good practice in the management of people with infertility problems, e.g. preventing side effects from treatments.
- Confidentiality: of information in consultations, in medical notes and between practitioners.
- Evidence-based practice and policy: applying it in practice, in the district, across the NHS.
- Accountability and performance: for standards, performance of individuals and the practice – to the public and those in authority.
- Core requirements: good fit with skill-mix and whether individuals are competent to do their jobs, communication, workforce numbers and morale at practice level.
- Health promotion: this might be opportunistic, or in general or targeting those with most needs. This might focus on lifestyle advice about sexual behaviour to prevent infertility for example.
- Audit and evaluation: for instance of the extent to which individuals and primary or secondary care teams adhere to best practice in clinical management.
- Risk management: being competent to spot those at risk; reducing risks and probabilities of ill health. This is particularly important in infertility practice where the complications from treatment can have serious consequences.

The challenges to delivering clinical governance

Delivering high quality healthcare with guaranteed minimum standards of care at all times is a major challenge. At present, the quality of healthcare is patchy and variable. We are not very good at detecting under-performance and rectifying it at an early stage. The small number of clinicians who do under-perform exert a disproportionately large effect on the public's confidence. Under-performance in an individual might be a result of a lack of knowledge or skills, poor attitude, ill health or a lack of resources. A lack of management capability is nearly always a contributory reason for inadequate clinical services.

We need to understand why variation exists and explore the ways of reducing inequalities. Variation in the quality of healthcare provided is common – between different practices in the same locality, between staff of the same discipline working in the same practice or unit, between care given to some groups of the population rather than others. For instance, not all general practices have written guidelines for referral of patients with fertility problems; and hospital protocols vary in the pathways of investigation and treatment they set out for those with infertility.

Clinical governance offers a co-ordinated approach to overcoming these areas of risk.[1] The complex cultural change that will be required to deliver uniformly excellent care is immense, and we need to develop measurable outcomes that professionals, patients and the public consider to be relevant and meaningful. We can then assess the progress made through implementing clinical governance.

Learning culture

Education and training programmes should be relevant to service needs, whether at organisational or individual levels. Continuing professional development (CPD) programmes need to meet both the learning needs of individual health professionals and the wider service development needs of the NHS. You should no longer opt for CPD activities according to what you *want* to do, but rather, what you *need* to do. Clinical governance underpins professional and service development.

---

individual personal development plans
will feed into a
workplace-based personal and professional development plan
that will feed into
the practice's/primary care organisation's or trust's business plan
all
underpinned by clinical governance[3]

So consider, introducing a regular multidisciplinary team meeting to bring together all those involved in providing care to patients or couples with infertility for an educational session. Review your protocols and agree the competencies each person needs to be able to play their full part – in clinical practice, counselling or managing the service. Is each member aware of the roles and responsibilities of the others? Are they merely competent or are they expert in their own roles, with a significant background experience and intuitive grasp of the diverse situations with which they may be presented?[4]

Applying research and development in practice

The findings of the many research papers about infertility published in reputable journals each year are rarely applied in practice. This is because few health professionals or managers read such journals regularly and are not aware of the research findings. Most general practices or hospital units do not have a system for reviewing important research papers and translating a review into practical action. Improvements should result if working parties can agree on local guideline templates such as for referrals, the management of infertility, recording data and making changes to working practices, provided such improvements are backed by resources.

> Incorporating research-based evidence into everyday practice should promote policies on effective working, improve quality and create a clinical governance culture.

Research increases understanding about the causes and effects of infertility as well as developing new treatments. It is widely thought that more research is needed into the effects of *in vitro* fertilisation (IVF) on the resulting child/ren and the welfare of any such child born as a result of infertility treatment. A disproportionate amount of research has concentrated on the needs and dilemmas of parents as opposed to the needs and feelings of the resulting children.

Therapeutic and human reproductive cloning are other allied areas of frontline research. The risks of human reproductive cloning are widely thought to outweigh the need for the research procedure to be permitted. There is considerable uncertainty about the potential child's interest and how the relationship between the parent and 'child' or rather, delayed twin, would develop.[5] Therapeutic cloning, however, is supported by the scientific community, as the embryonic stem cells that are produced are not allowed to develop into a foetus.

Research suggests that male factors are the commonest single defined cause of infertility.[6,7] Again, we need more follow-up research to identify any potential adverse effects on the long-term health of children conceived as a result of assisted reproductive techniques designed to overcome male factor infertility, such as the process of intracytoplasmic sperm injection (ICSI).

Reliable and accurate data

Clinicians, patients and administrators need access to reliable and accurate data. Set standards for your practice, whether it is in general practice or a hospital setting:

- keep records in chronological order
- summarise medical records, within a specified time period for records of new patients
- review dates for checks on medication and follow-up, with audit in place to monitor whether standards are adhered to, and plan for under-performance if necessary.
- use computers for diagnostic recording
- record information from external sources to your workplace – general practice, hospital, other organisations from NHS and private practice.

Keep good written records of policies and audits that relate to infertility. An HFEA inspection at any time should show what audits have been undertaken and when, the changes in practice or the organisation of systems and procedures that followed, the extent of staff training undertaken, and the future programme of monitoring care.

Well-managed resources and services

The things you need to achieve best practice should be in the right place at the right time and should work correctly every time.

Set standards in your practice or workplace for:

- access to premises and availability of services for people with special needs (such as those in wheelchairs)
- waiting times: provision of routine and urgent appointments, e.g. for those with symptoms of complications from treatment
- access to and provision for referral for investigation or treatment of infertility or an associated problem (e.g. depression if progress with infertility treatment is disappointing)
- alternatives to face-to-face consultations
- consultation length.

Systems should be designed to prevent and detect errors, so keep systems simple and sensible, and inform everyone how they operate so that they are less likely to bypass a system or make errors. Sort out good procedures for the follow-up of patients with infertility.

Co-ordinated teamwork

Effective teams make the most of the different contributions of individual clinical disciplines in delivering patient care. The characteristics of effective teams[8] are:

- shared ownership of a common purpose
- clear goals for the contribution each discipline makes
- open communication between team members
- opportunities for team members to enhance their skills.

A team approach helps different team members to adopt an evidence-based approach to patient care – by having to justify their approach to the rest of the team. The disciplines necessary for providing team-based care of those with infertility include the GP and practice nurse, non-clinical staff, junior doctors and hospital consultants, infertility specialist nurses, counsellors specialising in infertility practice and the community or hospital pharmacist, with expertise available from clinical geneticists, genetic counsellors and molecular biologists.

One study that evaluated the effect of clinical guidelines on the management of infertility across the primary–secondary care interface concluded that 'interventions are undermined if management in secondary care is not co-ordinated with that of primary care'. Those seeing patients in the hospital setting duplicated tests that had already been performed in primary care; there was no evidence that subsequent hospital management was improved as a result of better investigations carried out before referral.[9]

Meaningful involvement of patients and the public

People use terms such as 'user' or 'consumer' to describe who they should be involving in giving feedback about the quality or type of healthcare on offer, or in planning future services. Patients or carers, non-users of services, the local community, a particular subgroup of the population or the general public will all have useful feedback and views; for example, on your systems that inform people about the results of investigations or locating services closer to the patient.

The aims of user involvement and public participation include better outcomes of individual care and the health of the population, more locally responsive services and greater ownership of health services.[10] Those planning the services should develop a better understanding of why and how local services need to be changed. You might want to consult the public and health professionals about the closure of a community hospital, for example, or how healthcare resources are allocated, e.g. for infertility investigation and treatment.

Public consultation: on the whole, consultation exercises fail to reach most of the population. Some public opinion exercises are targeted at people or organisations who are already informed about the issues in question – see the illustration in the box below of the HFEA's public consultation on how banning payments to egg and sperm donors should be implemented.

Responses to the national public consultation on the implementation of withdrawal of payments to egg and sperm donors

The consultation paper was sent out to fertility centres and special interest groups across the UK; patients, the general public, clinic employees, health professionals and campaigners were all invited to respond. The consultation document contained background information about the topic and a mix of open and closed questions. The purpose of the exercise was to consult on how the HFEA's policy to end payments to donors might be implemented.

In the event, 176 completed questionnaires were returned, of which 154 were from individuals and 22 were corporate replies from organisations, groups or centres. Responses were mixed and ranged from wholehearted support for the HFEA's policy, to accusations that the policy to end payments was out of touch with the real world and the numbers of donors would be drastically

---

reduced as a result. Strong feeling spilled over outside the consultation to be expressed in the national press too. The question behind the consultation about how to implement the policy was widened by respondents into challenges to the actual policy itself, and included many other related issues, such as preserving the anonymity of donors, access to treatment, the ethics and practical considerations of egg sharing as a method of donation, and the importing/exporting of sperm to and from the UK.

As a result of the consultation and the HFEA's further reflections on the issue, the policy was softened and payments to donors of egg and sperm gametes were retained until acceptable alternatives were identified and introduced.

Patient involvement: patients may be involved as individuals in any part of the decision-making process of planning or providing healthcare for people with infertility. A single individual may have one extreme perspective, and so it is important to involve several or many patients in giving their views, by postal questionnaire, interviews, a focus group or possibly the Internet.

Patient satisfaction with infertility

A postal study undertaken to assess patient satisfaction with the investigation and initial management of infertility[11] found that:

- 86% felt they had not been given enough help with the emotional aspects of infertility
- 47% felt they had not been given a clear plan for the future
- 23% of those receiving drug treatments reported being given little or no information about the treatment or possible side effects.

Health gain

The two general approaches to improving health are the 'population' approach, focusing on measures to improve health through the community; and the 'high risk' approach, focusing on vulnerable individuals who are at a high risk of a condition or hazard.

The two approaches are not mutually exclusive and often need to be combined with legislation and community action. Health goals include:

- a good quality of life
- avoiding premature death
- equal opportunities for health.

Modifiable risk factors relevant to infertility and healthy pregnancy, identified by a 'population' approach, include:

- obesity
- lack of exercise
- smoking.

An example of the application of the 'high risk' approach in fertility practice is 'pre-implantation genetic diagnosis' for women whose babies are at risk of having a genetic condition serious enough for termination of their pregnancy to be considered. This involves testing the early embryo after IVF treatment at day three of its development. The test is used to detect the sex of the embryo for sex-linked disorders such as Duchenne muscular dystrophy, single gene defects such as cystic fibrosis, and chromosomal disorders.

Confidentiality

Confidentiality is a component of clinical governance that is often overlooked. Experienced health professionals and managers may assume that junior or new staff know all about confidentiality but, of course, they may not. There are many tricky situations in the NHS where one person asks for information about another's medical condition – for example, results of a couple's fertility tests requested by only one person of the couple – where it is not clear cut as to whether this information should be supplied or withheld.

The Caldicott committee report describes principles of good practice to safeguard confidentiality when information is being used for non-clinical purposes:[12]

- justify the purpose
- do not use patient-identifiable information unless it is absolutely necessary
- use the minimum necessary patient-identifiable information
- access to patient-identifiable information should be on a strict need-to-know basis
- everyone with access to patient-identifiable information should be aware of his or her responsibilities.

Evidence-based culture – policy and practice

The key features of whether or not local guidelines worked in one initiative[13] were that:

- there was multidisciplinary involvement in drawing them up
- a systematic review of the literature underpinned the guidelines, with graded recommendations for best practice linked to the evidence
- there was ownership at national and local levels
- a local implementation plan ensured that the need for resources, time, staff, education and training were foreseen, and met and supported
- plans were made to sustain the guidelines, which were user friendly and could be modified to suit individual practitioners and patients.

The hierarchy of evidence used to describe how scientifically a particular study was conducted, and therefore how reliable the conclusions are likely to be, varies between different reviews of published studies. There are several systems of grading evidence. A classification[14] that is often quoted gives the strength of evidence as shown in the box below.

Strength of evidence

Type I   Strong evidence from at least one systematic review of multiple well-designed randomised controlled trials (RCTs)

Type II   Strong evidence from at least one properly designed RCT of appropriate size

Type III Evidence from well-designed trials without randomisation, single group pre-post, cohort, time series or matched case-control studies

Type IV   Evidence from well-designed, non-experimental studies from ore than one centre or research group

Type V   Opinions of respected authorities, based on clinical evidence, descriptive studies or reports of expert committees

---

Other categories of evidence are listed in the compendium of the best available evidence for effective healthcare – *Clinical Evidence*[15] – which is updated every six months and is, perhaps, more useful to the health professional in everyday work.

Beneficial	Interventions whose effectiveness has been shown by clear evidence from controlled trials
Likely to be beneficial	Interventions for which effectiveness is less well established than for those listed under 'beneficial'
Trade off between benefits and harms	Interventions for which clinicians and patients should weigh up the beneficial and harmful effects according to individual circumstances and priorities
Unknown effectiveness	Interventions for which there are currently insufficient data or data of inadequate quality (includes interventions that are widely accepted as beneficial but have never been formally tested in RCTs, often because RCTs would be regarded as unethical)
Unlikely to be beneficial	Interventions for which lack of effectiveness is less well established than for those listed under 'likely to be ineffective or harmful'
Likely to be ineffective or harmful	Interventions whose ineffectiveness or harmfulness have been demonstrated by clear evidence

Accountability and performance

Health professionals who believe that they are not accountable to others may be reluctant to collect the evidence to demonstrate that they are fit to practise, and that their working environment is fit to practise from. They may be reluctant to co-operate with HFEA legislation in respect of the welfare of the child, for instance.

Identify and rectify under-performance at an early stage by, for example:

- regular appraisals (at least annually) linked into clinical governance and personal development plans as a process of regular supportive meetings between manager and staff member
- systematic audit that distinguishes individuals' performance from the overall performance of the practice team
- an open learning culture where team members are discouraged from covering up colleagues' inadequacies so that problems can be resolved at an early stage.

Health promotion

People with fertility problems will benefit if they are well informed and able to participate in making decisions about the management of their condition. Good information will help people make choices about their diet, smoking, physical activity and other health-related behaviour.

One study that examined the effects of alcohol consumption on the probability of conception found that women's alcohol intake did seem to influence their likelihood of conceiving. Women who consumed five or more drinks per week, seemed to be less likely to conceive than women who drank no alcohol. The authors of this study concluded that women who are trying to conceive should be encouraged to avoid alcohol.[16]

Audit and evaluation

Follow-up of those with fertility problems is critical to ensure that patients and couples are not lost from care through inefficient systems.

A national audit of infertility practices in primary care in Scotland in the mid-1990s showed the diverse range of practice and opinion held by GPs, which was often at odds with published scientific evidence. For instance, fewer than half of GPs agreed that 'temperature charts are of limited use and couples should be discouraged from completing them'. The findings fuelled the *local* development of evidence-based guidelines.[17]

Core requirements

You cannot deliver clinical governance without well-trained and competent staff, the right skill-mix of staff, a safe and comfortable working environment and providing cost-effective care.

A clinical governance culture addresses the recent challenges[1] in relation to:

- partnership: working together across the NHS to ensure the best possible care
- performance: acting to review and deliver higher standards of healthcare
- the professions and wider workforce: breaking down barriers between different disciplines, for instance though multidisciplinary teamwork between GPs and nurses, those working in primary care and secondary care sectors
- patient care: access, convenient services, empowerment to take a full part in decision making about their own medical care and in planning and providing health services in general
- prevention: promoting healthy living across all sections of society and tackling variations in care.

Risk management

People may under-estimate relative risks as applied to themselves and their own behaviour – for example, many smokers accept the relationship between smoking tobacco and disease, but do not believe that they are personally at risk. People usually have a reasonable idea of the *relative risks* of various activities and behaviours, although their personal estimates of the *magnitude* of risks tend to be biased – small probabilities are often over-estimated and high probabilities are often under-estimated.[18]

Risk management in healthcare centres mainly on assessing probabilities that potential or actual hazards will give rise to harm. Consider how bad is the risk, how likely is that risk, when will the risk happen, if ever, and how certain you are of estimates about the risks. This applies just as much whether the risk is an environmental or organisational risk in the practice, or a clinical risk.

Good practice means understanding and managing risk – both clinical and organisational aspects. Undertaking audit more systematically will reduce the risks of omission, such as viral contamination in storage banks.

Common areas of risk in providing healthcare services are:[13]

- out-of-date clinical practice
- lack of continuity of care
- poor communication
- mistakes in patient care
- patient complaints
- financial risk – insufficient resources
- reputation
- staff morale.

Communicating and managing risks on an individual basis with patients depends on finding ways to explain risks and elicit people's values and preferences. They can then make decisions themselves to take risks or choose between alternatives that involve different risks and benefits.

Another important form of risk in infertility practice might be of breaching ethical guidelines. The following extract from a national newspaper illustrates the importance of counselling, and ensuring that sperm donors are well counselled about the ethical implications of donation and not unduly influenced by the reimbursement of expenses, which to someone on a low income may seem like 'payment'.

In one article in a national newspaper, sperm donation was promoted to students as a good way to fund their studies in place of more traditional student jobs. Benjamin was described as having 'earned' about £450 as a sperm donor and was quoted as saying: 'It's not exactly the most strenuous work and I'd advise anybody to give it a go. As long as you have thought about the moral implications of it, then it is an easy way to make some money while you are at university . . . It's quite an enjoyable day out.'[19]

References

1 Chambers R and Wakley G (2000) *Making Clinical Governance Work For You*. Radcliffe Medical Press, Oxford.

2 Commission for Health Improvement (2000) *Clinical Governance Reviews. An overview*. CHI, London (leaflet).

3 Wakley G, Chambers R and Field S (2000) *Continuing Professional Development in Primary Care: making it happen*. Radcliffe Medical Press, Oxford.

4 Bennet P (1984) *From Novice to Expert*. Addison-Wesley, London.

5 Editorial (2001) Biological uncertainties about reproductive cloning. *Lancet*. **358**: 519.

6 Irvine DS (1998) Epidemiology and etiology of male infertility. *Hum Reprod*. **13**(supplement 1): 31–44.

7 Oehninger S (2001) Place of intracytoplasmic sperm injection in management of male infertility. *Lancet*. **357**: 2068–9.

8 Poulton B and West M (1999) The determinants of effectiveness in primary health care teams. *Journal of Interprofessional Care*. **13**(10): 7–18.

9 Morrison J, Carroll L, Twaddle S *et al*. (2001) Pragmatic randomised controlled trial to evaluate guidelines for the management of infertility across the primary care–secondary care interface. *BMJ*. **322**: 1282–4.

10 Chambers R (2000) *Involving Patients and the Public: How to do it better*. Radcliffe Medical Press, Oxford.

11 Souter VL, Penney G, Hopton JL *et al*. (1998) Patient satisfaction with the management of infertility. *Hum Reprod*. **113**(7): 1831–6.

12 Department of Health (1997) Report of the review of patient-identifiable information. In: *The Caldicott Committee Report*. Department of Health, London.

13 Donald P (2000) Promoting local ownership of guidelines. *Guidelines in Practice*. **3**: 17.

14 Muir Gray JA (1997) *Evidence-based Healthcare*. Churchill Livingstone, Edinburgh.

15 Barton S (ed) (2002) *Clinical Evidence*. Issue 7. BMJ Publishing Group, London.

16 Jensen TK, Hjollund NH, Henriksen TB *et al*. (1998) Does moderate alcohol consumption affect fertility? Follow up study among couples planning first pregnancy. *BMJ*. **317**: 505–10.

17 Souter VL, Penney G and Gorman D (1997) A survey of infertility practices in primary care in Scotland. *Br J Gen Pract*. **47**: 727–8.

18 Mohanna K and Chambers R (2001) *Risk Matters in Healthcare: Communicating, explaining and managing risk*. Radcliffe Medical Press, Oxford.

19 Gardner B (2001) Frozen donations bring in some cash. *The Times Higher.* **No 1500**: 15.

Reflection exercise

Exercise 1: Review your clinical management of people with infertility problems

Think how you might integrate the 14 components of clinical governance into your personal development plan. Examples are given for each component listed below. Complete this yourself from your own perspective.

- *Establishing a learning culture*: e.g. informal discussion about infertility guidelines between GPs, nurses and the team from the local fertility treatment centre.
- *Managing resources and services*: e.g. review the role and responsibilities of members of the team and attached staff for managing infertility practices.
- *Establishing a research and development culture*: e.g. share findings in key research papers on best practice in managing aspects of infertility among your team.
- *Reliable and accurate data*: e.g. keep electronic records (self and team) so that everyone uses the same computerised codes and enters data consistently. Any audit exercises can be repeated next year and results compared.
- *Evidence based practice and policy*: e.g. update evidence-based protocol for fertility investigation and treatments.
- *Confidentiality*: e.g. review that everyone is adhering to the code of practice for giving results or advice at reception – in the practice or hospital ward.
- *Health gain*: e.g. target particular patients for special efforts in reducing their risk factors thus reducing their chances of conceiving or having healthy pregnancies.
- *Coherent team*: e.g. communicate new systems for detecting complications of treatment to the rest of the team.
- *Audit and evaluation*: e.g. undertake an audit and act on the findings to improve quality of care.
- *Meaningful involvement of patients and the public*: e.g. listen to and

act on the comments of those with fertility problems about the care and services you are providing.

- *Health promotion*: e.g. obtain or write literature promoting stopping smoking for women who are planning to conceive or who are already pregnant.
- *Risk management*: e.g. establish systems and procedures to identify, analyse and control clinical risks, such as those from careless repeat prescribing practices.
- *Accountability and performance*: e.g. keep good records of those with fertility problems to demonstrate best practice in the prevention of complications and clinical management.
- *Core requirements*: e.g. agree roles and responsibilities in the team, such as when nurses should refer to GPs or GPs refer to hospital specialists.

Now that you have completed this interactive reflection exercise transfer the information to the empty template of the personal development plan on pages 122 to 129 if you are working on your own learning plan. Don't forget to keep the evidence of your learning in your personal portfolio.

Part Two:
The problem of infertility

CHAPTER 2

An overview of infertility

How common is infertility?

Around one in six couples experiencing difficulties conceiving a child[1-3] seek specialist help at some time in their lives. The increased numbers of people presenting for help with infertility may have given a false impression that infertility is becoming more common, when there has probably been little change in prevalence over recent years.[1] It is widely

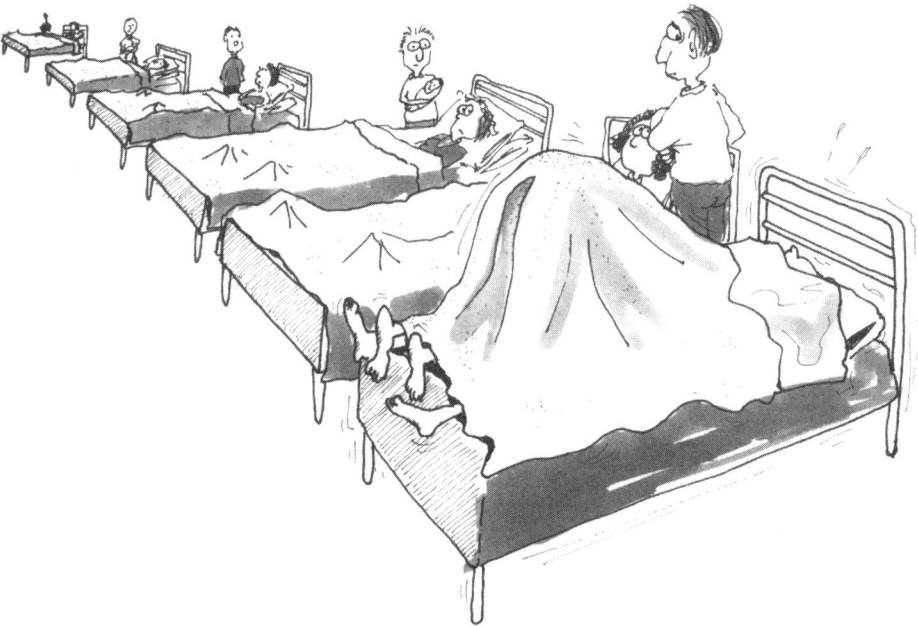

One in six couples seek
help for conceiving.

held that sperm counts are falling dramatically, but a recent review[4] has shown that the findings of published surveys may have been wrongly interpreted, as far as countries other than the USA are concerned.

Although there may be no increase in the prevalence of infertility, there appears to be a trend towards more patients seeking help with infertility problems.[5] This increasing demand may be due to the major developments in the management of infertility, which have attracted media interest. Postal questionnaires dividing infertility into primary infertility, where the couples have never achieved a pregnancy, and secondary infertility, where they have previously achieved a pregnancy, suggested that around 16% of couples after one year and 9% of couples after two years experience primary infertility.[5,6] These studies suggested that a further 16% of couples after one year and 5% of couples after two years experience secondary infertility. One report suggested that at some time during their reproductive period, around one in four couples may seek advice about infertility from their GP,[5] although a report in 1984 suggested that only one in six couples visited hospital specialists.[2] The true scale of infertility may be even greater, as the rate of infertility in couples responding to postal questionnaires may not be the same as that in couples who do not reply to questionnaires, and may be higher in subgroups such as couples delaying the start of their family.

By studying records of births, marriages and deaths from prior to the introduction of effective contraception, Menken and Larsen[7] provided a guide to natural fertility related to age. Intercourse was assumed to begin at the time of marriage and only women who survived until at least 50 years were considered. Figure 2.1 shows that fertility starts to fall significantly at 35 years of age, and falls steeply beyond 40 years.

About half of couples having regular unprotected intercourse will

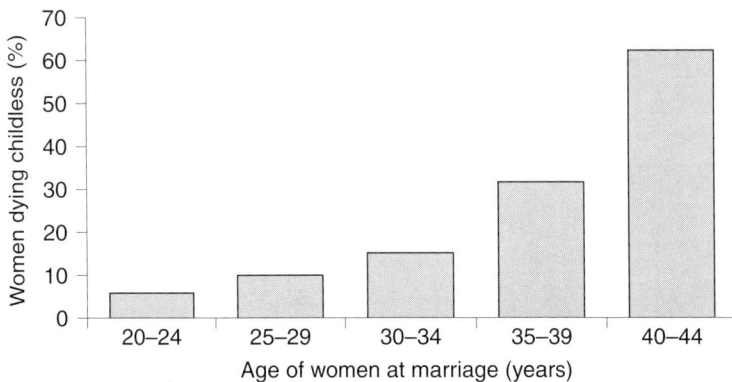

Figure 2.1: Risk of childlessness for women related to age at marriage.

have conceived within three months, two-thirds by six months and 90% by 12 months.[8] The definition of 'subfertility' is 'failure to conceive within one year of unprotected intercourse'.[8] Although perhaps not strictly correct, the term 'infertility' has come to be synonymous with 'subfertility' in routine practice.

The chance of achieving pregnancy each month reduces steadily with time, as illustrated by Zinaman's study of women discontinuing contraception with the aim of becoming pregnant (*see* Figure 2.2).[9] By reviewing over 2000 infertile couples, Collins produced a guide to the chances of achieving pregnancy without treatment (*see* Table 2.1).[10] The baseline cumulative pregnancy rate is modified by applying each multiplication factor that applies to the couple, thus providing an individualised chance of pregnancy. For instance, if a couple had one prior pregnancy, multiplying the baseline rate by 1.8 would increase their cumulative live birth rate. If a couple had a prior pregnancy and had endometriosis, then the baseline rate would be multiplied by 1.8 times 0.4. This mathematical model has been applied to an easy-to-use 'Fertility Calculator', which is available on a website for anyone to use themselves (www.ReproMED.co.uk).

Causes of infertility

There is a huge spectrum of causes of infertility. These include failure to ovulate, failure to produce or deliver adequate numbers of healthy sperm to the fallopian tubes, obstruction in the fallopian tubes,

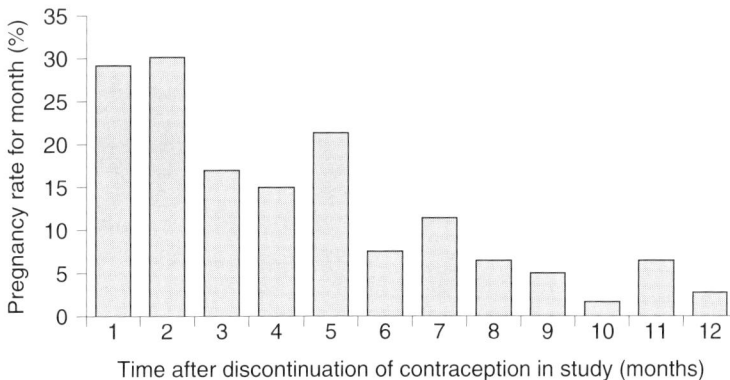

Figure 2.2: Chance of achieving a pregnancy after discontinuing contraception.

Table 2.1: A guide to prognosis for pregnancy without fertility treatment[10]

Average baseline prognosis

Months	Cumulative live birth rate (%)
3	4.2
6	8.1
12	14.3
24	21.2
36	25.2

Effects of prognostic factors

Prognostic factor	Multiplication factor
Prior pregnancy in partnership	1.8
Duration of infertility < 36 months	1.7
Female age < 30 years	1.5
Male defect	0.5
Endometriosis	0.4
Tubal defect	0.5

endometriosis or adhesions involving the ovaries or fallopian tubes, previous or current infections in the reproductive tracts of male or female, poor timing or technique of sexual intercourse, an unreceptive lining in the uterus repelling implantation, immunological barriers to fertilisation or implantation, genetic factors, chemotherapy or other drugs, secondarily caused by physiological factors such as weight loss or excessive exercise, or from other causes of gonadotrophin disorder connected, for example, with hyperprolactinaemia, a pituitary tumour or polycystic ovary syndrome.

Causes of subfertility vary according to socio-economic and geographic factors. A minor cause of subfertility in both the male and female partners can combine to a more major problem of subfertility as a couple.[11] Polycystic ovary syndrome is more common than used to be thought and may be associated with lowered fertility in some cases.

In addition to regional variations, there are significant differences between centres in the extent of investigation of the couple and differences in the definitions used. Nevertheless, Collins' review of attendees to Canadian infertility clinics provides a good idea of the relative importance of the main causes of infertility (*see* Figure 2.3).[10]

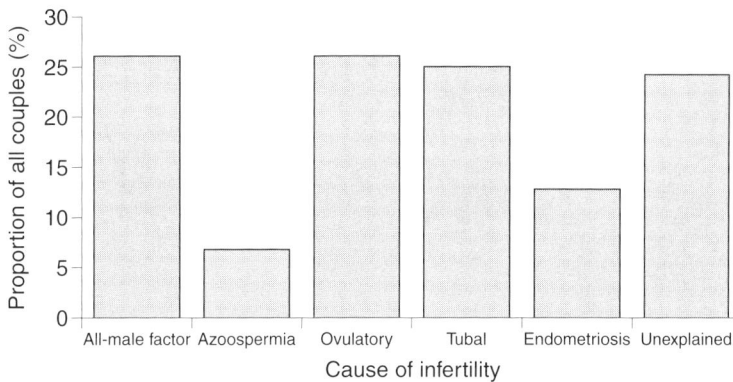

Figure 2.3: Relative occurence of major causes of infertility.

Genital tract infection with *Chlamydia trachomatis* is a major risk factor for subsequent tubal infertility.[12] Unfortunately, tubal infection with *Chlamydia* can be asymptomatic, and those with symptoms are often a small proportion of those affected.[12] The feasibility of general practice-based opportunistic screening in sexually active women under 25 years and high risk older women is currently being piloted. The numbers of cases of *Chlamydia* infection are soaring, with a 106% increase in the numbers of cases in England and Wales between 1995 and 2000, according to the Public Health Laboratory Service. The rise in numbers of *Chlamydia* infection is probably due as much to increased detection by GPs and other clinicians who have become increasingly aware of the possibility of *Chlamydia* infection being present and tested for it accordingly, as it is to increased prevalence.

Box 2.1: Causes of female infertility

- Tubal damage: from sexually transmitted diseases, complications of coil, any sepsis
- Primary ovarian failure
- Secondary ovarian failure – effects of age, premature menopause
- Polycystic ovarian syndrome
- Hypogonadotrophic hypogonadism – deficiency of follicle-stimulating hormone (FSH) and luteinising hormone (LH)
- Hyperprolactinaemia, from pituitary adenoma
- Endometriosis
- Intrauterine fibroids, polyps
- Significant systemic illness
- Previous sterilisation

Box 2.2: Causes of male infertility

- Deficient spermatogenesis – congenital (e.g. Klinefelter's syndrome) or acquired (for example, chemotherapy)
- Previous vasectomy
- Antisperm antibodies
- Hypogonadotrophic hypogonadism – deficiency of FSH and LH
- Hyperprolactinaemia, from pituitary adenoma
- Ejaculation disorders, for example retrograde ejaculation, impotence
- Obstruction to outflow of sperm
- Significant systemic illness

Licensed and unlicensed treatment options

The range of treatment options for reversing infertility includes the use of fertility drugs in men and women to induce ovulation or improve hormone or sperm production, surgery to the male or female reproductive tracts to remove blockages or abnormalities, insemination of sperm and assisted reproduction – most commonly, IVF and ICSI. Surrogacy or third-party reproduction for women without a uterus is also a possibility.

Some fertility treatments require a licence, in accordance with the legal directions in the Human Fertilisation and Embryology Act (HF&E Act), passed in 1990. Any treatment that involves the creation, keeping and using of human embryos outside the body, or the storage or donation of human eggs and sperm, is a licensable activity. Insemination of a woman with her husband's or partner's sperm while he is alive is not regulated by the HF&E Act because insemination and fertilisation occur inside the woman's body and the man and woman are being treated together. That is why gamete intra-fallopian transfer (GIFT) using the partner's sperm does not require a licence while IVF does. Unlike IVF, GIFT does not involve handling gametes and creating embryos in a laboratory outside the human body, so GIFT can be offered by district general hospital trusts that do not have a specialised fertility treatment service. There is controversy about the fact that GIFT is not covered by the HF&E Act despite the procedure incurring similar medical, social and ethical risks to IVF.

These licensed fertility treatments are invasive and it is all too easy for couples longing for a baby to rush into the ultimate assisted conception technology rather than wait a little longer for spontaneous conception to occur or try simpler treatments first.

The Human Fertilisation and Embryology Authority (HFEA)

The Human Fertilisation and Embryology Authority was set up to regulate and license infertility treatment in accordance with the HF&E Act in 1990, following the recommendations of the Warnock report in 1984. It grants licences to fertility clinics for treatment and storage of eggs, sperm and embryos, monitors and encourages good practice, maintains a database of treatments given, publishes information and describes centres' success rates, regulates research on embryos and regularly reports to, and advises, the Secretary of State for Health.

Besides licensing any assisted conception techniques involving donated eggs or sperm, the HFEA also licenses the storage of human eggs, sperm or embryos for treatment or research.

Research is limited to embryos up to 14 days after fertilisation has occurred. The HFEA Licence committees scrutinise research applications to ensure that the use of human embryos is essential for the purposes of research. This means that the numbers of embryos used should be kept to a minimum in any research protocol and that the proposed studies should not duplicate other published work unnecessarily.

The HFEA runs a website (www.hfea.gov.uk) and publishes a variety of information leaflets, reports and consultation documents for the public. Videos on IVF and donor insemination (DI) are available for educational purposes. Further details about titles and availability are given at the back of the book.

The HFEA does not license all fertility treatment and does not play any part in resource allocation and the differential NHS funding of fertility treatments around the UK. Although the HFEA likes to hear about patients' complaints, it does not act as an ombudsman or have any official role.

The overriding importance of the welfare of the child

Clinicians considering whether to provide couples with licensed fertility treatment are required to take account of 'the welfare of any child who may be born as a result of treatment (including the need of that child for a father) and of any other child who may be affected by the birth' [Section 13 (5) of the HF&E Act, 1990]. The child or children who 'may be affected' are any others within the potential child's household or family. The legal requirement to consider the welfare of the prospective child applies to all licensed fertility treatments and all unlicensed treatments at licensed fertility centres, and is good practice for all fertility treatment. In practice, this means that all licensed fertility clinics must be able to demonstrate that they are adhering to their written protocols for assessing the welfare of any potential children. They should check who will be legally responsible for the child and the suitability of those intending to bring the child up, to be sure that there is a stable and supportive environment awaiting any child born as a result of fertility treatment (*see* Box 2.3 for more details).

Licensed clinics are required to check out past medical and social histories of the intending parents with their GP to make sure that there are no pre-existing reasons why they would not make suitable parents and that they are physically healthy and fit enough for a pregnancy. Some GPs resent these enquiries, and feel that making such judgements is discriminatory against the infertile, as society does not assess the suitability of parents who conceive naturally, and that doctors are not in a position to judge other people's suitability as prospective parents (*see* Box 2.4, p. 35).

Before commencing assisted conception treatment in the UK it is obligatory to conduct a careful assessment of the welfare of the unborn child. This assessment will include asking the patients relevant questions and seeking the views of their GPs. Typically, if any issues of concern are raised, the senior clinic staff will discuss these, taking advice from an independent ethics committee where appropriate. Should a decision be made not to proceed with treatment then the couple would be informed of this decision sensitively and counselling offered.

Clinicians considering treating older couples 'must bear in mind the welfare of the potential child when deciding whether or not to provide treatment. This includes both the parents' ages and their likely ability

---

Box 2.3: Factors to be considered about prospective parents and the welfare of the child, of which centres should be aware where people are seeking licensed treatment (HFEA Code of Practice[13]):

- their commitment to bringing up a child or children
- their ability to provide a stable and supportive environment for any child produced as a result of treatment
- their medical histories and the medical histories of their families
- their health and consequent future ability to look after or provide for a child's needs
- their ages and likely future ability to look after and provide for a child's needs
- their ability to meet the needs of any child or children who may be born as a result of treatment, including the implications of any possible multiple births
- any risk of harm to the child or children who may be born, including the risk of inherited disorders or transmissible diseases, problems during pregnancy and of neglect or abuse
- the effect of a new baby or babies upon any existing child of the family.

Reproduced from the HFEA's Code of Practice, 2001, with their permission.

---

to look after and provide for a child in the future, the need of a child for a father, and the possible attitudes of other members of the family towards the child'.[14]

Most clinics treat women up until the age they might naturally be able to give birth. Some clinics interpret this upper age as being 45 years, but there are instances of women of up to 55 years being assisted with conception. In one survey, 12 clinics confirmed that their upper age limit for treatment for women was 50 years.[15] The HFEA 'would investigate any clinic that appeared to be routinely treating women in their fifties and has done so in the past'. But the (HFEA's) concern has always been with the process by which clinics reach their decisions rather than about the individual decisions themselves. Only a small proportion of women who receive licensed fertility treatment are in the older age groups – only 62 cycles of DI, 32 micromanipulation cycles and 202 cycles of IVF treatments were carried out on women aged 45 years and over, in the UK over a 12-month period to March 1997, which is less than 1% of all licensed

---

Box 2.4: An exchange of correspondence describing one GP's perspective of a routine enquiry as to a patient's suitability to be a parent and the response:

'I don't feel able or willing to sign a form that, in essence, asks for a judgement from me on the suitability of a woman to become a mother. No such permission is required for natural conception, and who am I to say that someone is or is not "suitable" to become a mother? Hitler I think would argue differently which is the whole point.'

And the reply:

'. . . Although there is no legal requirement for GPs to respond to these requests, the provision of information by a GP greatly assists the clinician offering treatment to come to a decision. However as you will see from Section 3 of the HFEA's Code of Practice[13] ["Centres should seek to satisfy themselves that the GP of each prospective parent knows of no reason why either of them might not be suitable for the treatment to be offered. This would include anything which might adversely affect the welfare of any resulting child."] the response that you give only forms part of the clinician's assessment. You and your GP colleagues are not absolutely "vouching" for a couple's suitability. It is the clinician at the licensed centre who must take responsibility for the decision to offer treatment.'

---

fertility treatment.[16] The oldest woman to have been treated by IVF was 60 years of age, according to the HFEA's register of details; the patient gave birth at 61 years old, having reportedly misled the fertility clinic about her real age.

The HF&E Act (1990) does not exclude any particular category of women from receiving licensed treatment. The case of a single woman seeking treatment should be considered on its own merits, and the final decision as to whether to provide treatment will rest with the clinician concerned, taking into account the HFEA's Code of Practice.[14] Where there is no father, fertility clinics should assess the prospective mother's ability to meet the child's needs throughout childhood, and what other family and friends will be involved in bringing the child up. That means that it is possible for single women or one partner of a lesbian couple to undergo assisted conception if they fulfil these conditions. However, in practice, the HFEA records show that the treatment of single women is uncommon, with there being no male partner recorded for less than 1% of all treatment cycles undertaken by UK fertility clinics.

Human Rights Act 1998[17]

It is not yet known how this Act will affect infertility practice. However, clinics must take the Act into account when assessing individuals for treatment. Box 2.5 includes the Articles that are relevant.

Box 2.5: Articles relevant to infertility treatment in the Human Rights Act

Article 2   Right to life
Article 6   Right to a fair trial
Article 8   Right to respect for private and family life
Article 12   Right to marry
Article 14   Prohibition of discrimination, when interpreting the above articles

---

References

1 Royal College of Obstetricians and Gynaecologists (1998) *The initial investigation and management of the infertile couple. Evidence-based clinical guidelines. No. 2.* Royal College of Obstetricians and Gynaecologists, London.

2 Hull M, Glazener C, Kelly N *et al.* (1985) Population study of causes, treament, and outcome of infertility. *BMJ.* **291**: 1693–7.

3 Braudet P and Ledger W (1998) *Infertility into the Millennium.* National Infertility Awareness Campaign, London.

4 Becker S and Birhane K (1997) A meta-analysis of 61 sperm count studies revisited. *Fertility and Sterility.* **67**: 1103–8.

5 Gunnell DJ and Ewings P (1994) Infertility prevalence, needs assessment and purchasing. *J Publ Health Med.* **16**: 29–36.

6 Templeton A, Fraser C and Thompson B (1990) The epidemiology of infertility in Aberdeen. *BMJ.* **301**: 148–52.

7 Menhen J and Larrsen U (1986) Guide to natural fertility with age. In: Mastroianni L and Paulsen A (eds) *Aging, Reproduction and the Climaiteric.* Plenum, New York.

8 Johnson M and Everitt B (1997) *Essential Reproduction.* Blackwell, Oxford.

9 Zinaman M, O'Connor J, Clegg ED *et al.* (1996) Estimates of human fertility and pregnancy loss. *Fertile Steril.* **65**: 503–9.

10 Collins J, Burrows E and Willan A (1995) The prognosis for live birth among untreated infertile couples. *Fertil Steril.* **64**: 22–8.

11 Royal College of Obstetricians and Gynaecologists (1998) *The management of infertility in secondary care. Evidence-based clinical guidelines. No. 3.* Royal College of Obstetricians and Gynaecologists, London.

12 Winter A and Ahmad S (1998) Managing infertility in general practice must include screening for sexual infections. *BMJ.* **317**: 1526 (letter).

13 Human Fertilisation and Embryology Authority (2001) *Code of Practice.* HFEA, London.

14 Press release, 11 September 1998. HFEA, London.

15 Furse A (1997) *Infertility Companion: a user's guide to tests, technologies and therapies.* Thorsons, London.

16 Human Fertilisation and Embryology Authority (1998) *Annual Report 1998.* HFEA, London.

17 Human Rights Act (1998). HMSO, London.

Reflection exercises

Exercise 2

If you are working in primary care, use the first chapter as a spur to find out whether there are data in your practice about the number of patients who have presented with infertility problems, the number subsequently referred and the outcomes of investigation and treatment.

- Do you need to improve the quality of the data you collect about your patient population?
- Could you and others in the practice be more systematic about recording data about patients' clinical conditions?

Exercise 3

If you are working in general practice or hospital, were you surprised by the increase in frequency of *Chlamydia* infection? Do you know how many of the patients you see for infertility have previously contracted *Chlamydia*? Is there anything more you could do to prevent other patients from contracting *Chlamydia* (e.g. health promoting activities to individuals, via media, etc.)?

Now that you have completed these interactive reflection exercises transfer the information to the empty template of the personal development plan on pages 122 to 129 if you are working on your own learning plan. Don't forget to keep the evidence of your learning in your personal portfolio.

Part Three:
Managing infertility in general practice

CHAPTER 3

The GP's eye view of the symptoms and signs

Assess both male and female partners of the couple present-ing with subfertility.

In the woman

In the woman **ask about:** personal and lifestyle details – age, the extent of stress in her life, whether she takes strenuous exercise, her smoking status, her usual alcohol intake, current and recent occupations, the frequency of sexual intercourse and the length of unprotected inter-course.

Medical details: menstrual history – whether she has suffered from amenorrhoea (absent periods) or oligomenorrhoea (irregular periods) and whether any previous pregnancies were with the same or other partners, previous abdominal or pelvic surgery, previous sexually transmitted disease or pelvic inflammatory disease (PID), previous abnormal tests such as a cervical smear, rubella status, previous contraceptive history, her current medication including recreational drugs, and any systemic or debilitating illnesses including anorexia nervosa. The drug compounds that have been associated with adverse effects on fertility or sexual function[1] include: non-steroidal anti-inflammatory drugs, some chemotherapeutic agents and cannabis.

Look for: obesity (body mass index $\geqslant 30$) or underweight or abnorm-alities in the pelvic examination to give clues to the cause of sub-fertility, such as vaginal infection or pain indicating endometriosis or PID. Previous treatment for abnormal smears may have caused cervical stenosis. Bimanual examination may reveal an ovarian cyst or fibroids. Hirsutism and/or acne may be the clue to the presence of polycystic ovarian syndrome. Galactorrhoea will suggest the probability of hyper-prolactinaemia.

In the man

In the man **ask about:** personal and lifestyle details – age, his smoking status, his usual alcohol intake, current and recent occupations, the frequency of sexual intercourse and the length of unprotected inter-course. Relevant details include exposure to agricultural chemicals such as pesticides, X-rays, and chemicals used in the preparation of solvents and heavy metals, which have been shown to adversely effect sperm quality and/or quantity. Evidence suggests that an increased testicular temperature may decrease sperm count and quality, and occupational and social circumstances such as working as a welder, sitting in a wheelchair or wearing tight trousers may be relevant to a history of male subfertility.[1] Showers and saunas do not increase the intrascrotal temperature, but soaking in a hot bath might do so.[2]

Medical details: any previous sexually transmitted diseases, any previous (uro)genital pathology or treatment, any systemic or debilitat-ing illnesses and whether there have been previous pregnancies with the same or other partners. Record drug history – although certain medication, particularly sildenofil citrate, may have a beneficial action on sexual function, other medication may cause impotence or reduce sperm production. Some medications may reduce the sperm count, reduce libido or impair the ability to achieve an erection. These include:

- drugs for high blood pressure, e.g. reserpine, methyldopa, guanethi-dine and propranolol
- certain antibiotics, e.g. sulphasalazine, nitrofurantoin and tetra-cyclines
- corticosteroids
- anti-psychotic drugs, e.g. phenathiazines, tricyclic antidepressants and monoamine oxidase inhibitors
- others, e.g. cimetidine, allopurinol and ketoconazole
- anabolic steroids for muscle building
- recreational drugs (cannabis, cocaine)
- some anti-cancer drugs and radiation therapy (remember that sperm may be frozen and stored before treatment).

Look for: any genital abnormality such as small soft testes, a lump within the testis which might be testicular cancer, or an undescended testis; and assess secondary sex characteristics. About 25% of those seeking assessment for infertility have a varicocele.[3] There is conflict-ing evidence about whether a varicocele is a cause of infertility that may be improved by surgery; if the sperm count is very low, surgery is unlikely to be helpful.

References

1 Royal College of Obstetricians and Gynaecologists (1998) *The initial investigation and management of the infertile couple. Evidence-based clinical guidelines. No.* 2. Royal College of Obstetricians and Gynaecologists, London.

2 Brindley GS (1982) Deep scrotal temperature and the effect on it of clothing, air temperature, activity, posture and paraplegia. *Br J Urol.* **54**: 49–55.

3 Hargreave T and Mills J (1998) Investigating and managing infertility in general practice. *BMJ.* **316**: 1438–41.

Reflection exercise

Exercise 4

Undertake an audit of patients and couples with infertility who have been referred to specialist care (e.g. ten patients/couples).

- Have you recorded their current smoking status?
- Has the status of the woman's immunity to rubella been checked and is this recorded in her medical records? If she is not immune, has appropriate action been taken to vaccinate her and re-test her six weeks later?
- Has the body mass index of the patient/couples been calculated? If so, have any patients whose BMI is ⩾ 30 received appropriate advice? Have these patients subsequently lost weight as recorded in follow-up medical notes?
- Is the full history of previous pregnancies in the notes, including those with a previous partner?
- What information and support have they been given? Have they received counselling? Are you happy with the quality of care they have received so far? On what are you basing the standards of quality?

Now that you have completed this interactive reflection exercise transfer the information to the empty template of the personal development plan on pages 122 to 129 if you are working on your own learning plan. Don't forget to keep the evidence of your learning in your personal portfolio.

CHAPTER 4

Initial management by the GP

Figure 4.1 shows the key stages in investigating and managing the infertile couple in primary care, from taking a history at initial representation, to examining both partners and carrying out a few simple tests, and then deciding whether and when it is appropriate to refer them to a fertility specialist.

Advice and checks

- Check the rubella status in the woman. Seronegative women should have a rubella vaccination and avoid pregnancy by using effective contraception until repeat serology confirms rubella immunity six weeks later.
- Advise women who are trying to conceive to take folic acid as a dietary supplement, which should be continued until 12 weeks of any pregnancy. The recommended dose is normally 0.4 mg a day, or 4 mg daily in those women who have previously had a child with a neural tube defect or are taking anti-epileptic medication.[1]
- Provide details of organisations to which the infertile couple may apply for information about infertility, different types of treatment, and the relative advantages of different clinics and centres (see Appendix 1).
- Advise both partners to stop smoking if either or both are smokers. Stopping smoking improves the woman's fertility and reduces the chances of a miscarriage if she does conceive.[1] Smoking in men is known to affect sperm quality in that smokers' sperm concentration is on average 13–17% lower than that of non-smokers, which may be particularly important in subfertile men with lowish sperm concentrations.
- Recommend women to limit their alcohol intake to no more than

Couple present with infertility → **Check if there is local protocol**

REMEMBER

Remember
- Female rubella status
- Folic acid
- If female BMI > 30 advise weight loss
- Drug history
- Occupational history
- Cervical smear history

← **History and examination of both partners** →

- Advise regular intercourse two or three times a week
- **Do not** use basal body temperature charts or LH detection kits

Advice to both partners on smoking and drinking

FEMALE   **MALE**

HISTORY

Consider early referral if:
- Aged over 35 years
- Amenorrhoea/oligomenorrhoea
- Previous abdo/pelvic surgery
- Previous PID/STD
- Abnormal pelvic exam

Consider early referral if:
- Previous genital pathology
- Previous urogenital surgery
- Previous STD
- Varicocele
- Significant systemic illness
- Abnormal genital exam

TESTS

- Confirm ovulation with mid-luteal progesterone level
- **Do not** measure thyroid function or prolactin if regular cycles

- Arrange for two semen analyses to be sent to laboratory used by clinic to which patient is referred

Discuss results with couple and plan future management

REFERRAL

If any test results abnormal refer to dedicated specialist infertility clinic

Can defer referral if history, examination and investigations normal in both partners and duration of infertility < 18 months

Plan for ongoing support in primary care after referral

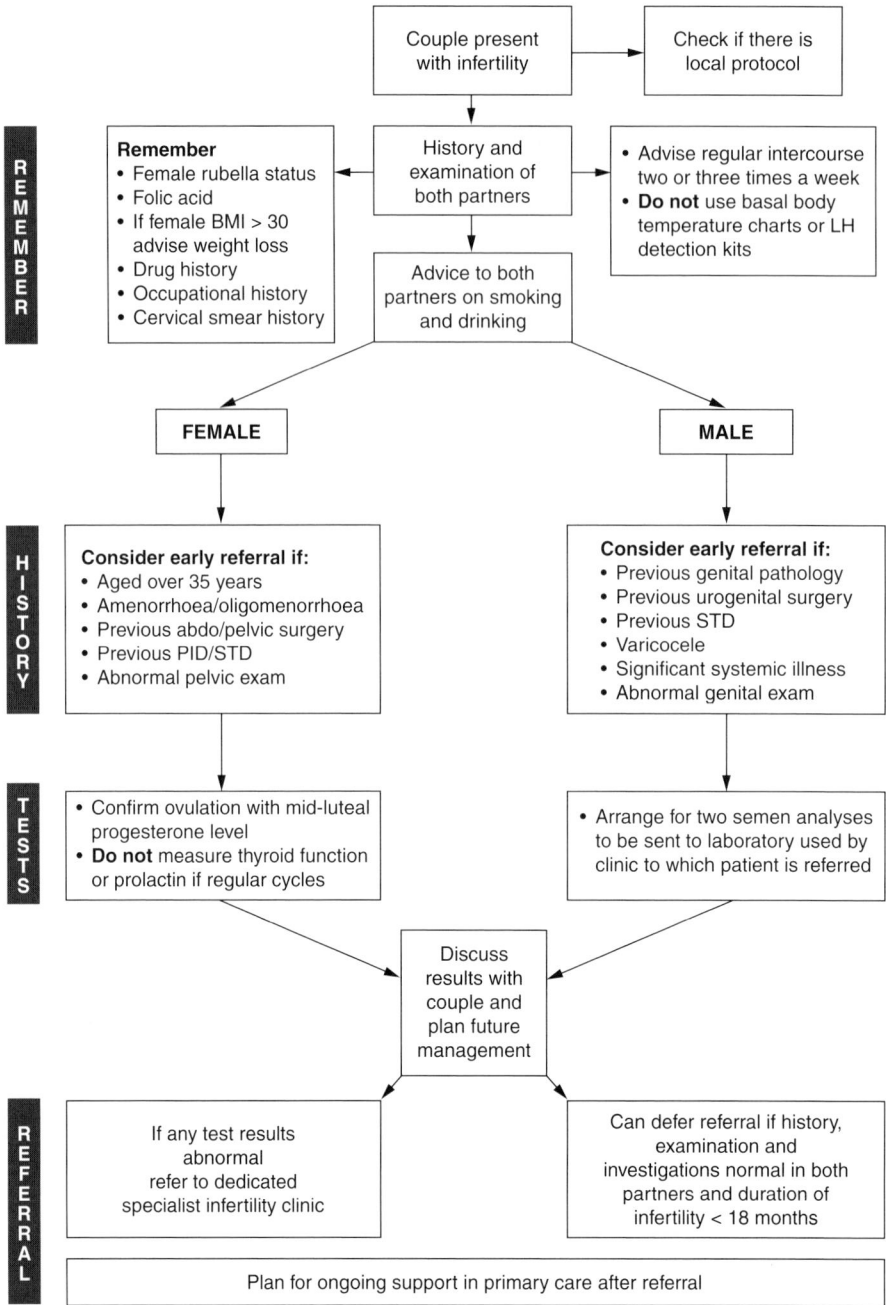

Figure 4.1: The investigation and management of the infertile couple in primary care. (Reprinted with permission from the Royal College of Obstetricians and Gynaecologists (1998) *Evidence-based Clinical Guidelines No. 2.* RCOG, London.[1])

one unit of alcohol a day and preferably one or two units once or twice a week, while trying to conceive.[1,2] Until there is more evidence about the link between alcohol and female infertility and fetal development this is the advice advocated by the Royal College of Obstetricians and Gynaecologists and the then-Health Education Authority.[3] Similarly for men, evidence linking excess alcohol and male infertility is inconclusive and the experts' advice is to moderate drinking to three or four units or less of alcohol a day.[1]

- Encourage women who are obese, weighing in with body mass indices of 30 or more, to lose weight. Moderate weight loss may restore ovulation and improve pregnancy rates.[3] One study of 67 overweight women with infertility problems showed that fertility improved after they had lost an average of 10 kg. Obesity in men has not been shown to be linked with subfertility.[1]
- Urge couples to continue to have regular sexual intercourse rather than strictly timing intercourse around the woman's periods.
- Look for clues of any underlying psychosexual problems. Associated problems are common in the presentation of any gynaecological problem.
- Explore and address the couple's fears and anxieties about the infertility, and remember that they will still need support while under specialist infertility care. There are a lot of myths around about infertility and even the most intelligent patients can have seemingly illogical beliefs about the causes or effects of their infertility. A survey of patient satisfaction in patients attending outpatient fertility clinics found that half the respondents reported that they had not been given a clear plan for the future, and a quarter had received little or no information about their drug treatment or its side effects.[4]

Is it true that . . .?

- Stress causes difficulties in conceiving? Although the hypothalamus regulates ovarian function via the pituitary, it is probably only in extreme circumstances that stress affects fertility.[5]
- Taking the woman's temperature first thing in the morning and using temperature charts to detect ovulation can be counterproductive? Yes – basal body temperature charts are not good at predicting ovulation and trying to time intercourse can be emotionally stressful.[4]
- There is no need to measure prolactin in women presenting with a regular menstrual cycle and infertility? Yes – this test is only indicated in women with an irregular menstrual cycle or

There are many causes of infertility; losing weight may help in more ways than one!

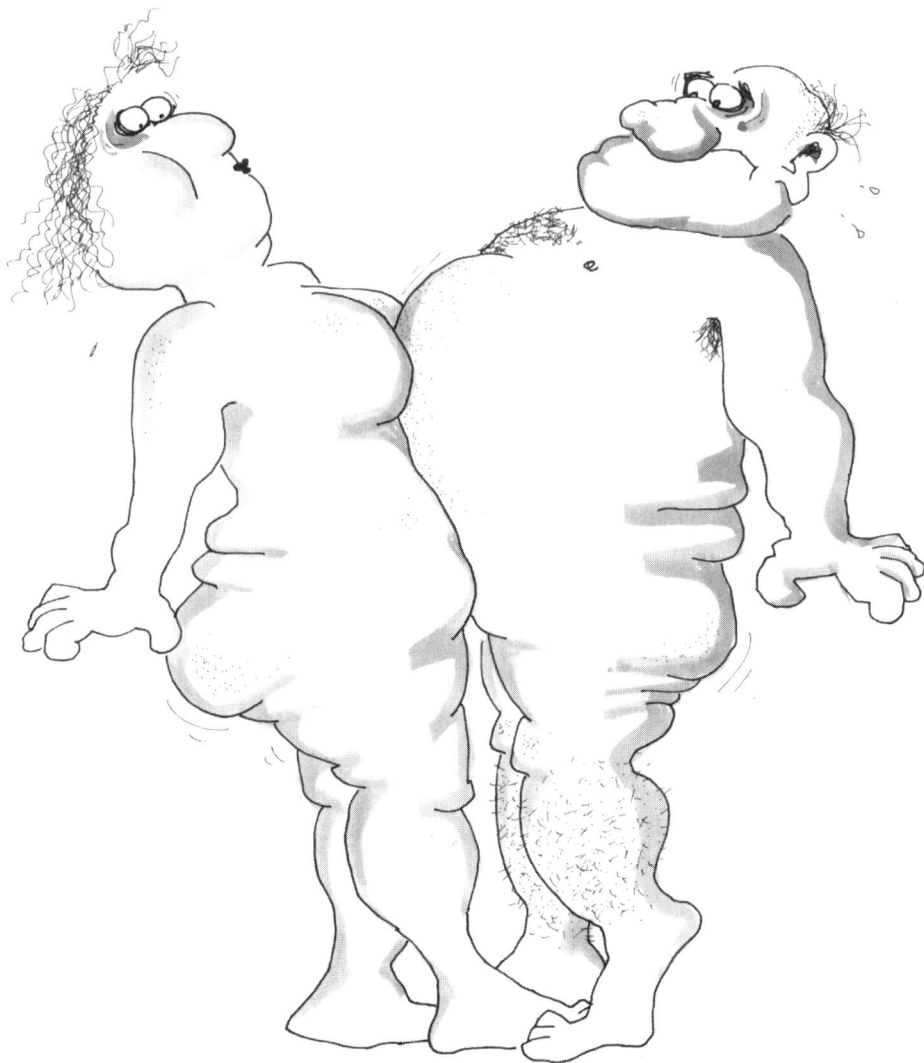

"Come on darling—it's the **right** time of the month tonight!"

galactorrhora. Thyroid function tests should be measured if there is any suggestion of thyroid disease. Many specialists check this routinely, although RCOG guidelines state that routine testing is unnecessary.[1]

Box 4.1

A biology teacher confidently informed the clinic nurse that she could only have boy babies in future as she had had what she assumed was the 'girl egg' ovary removed when she had had an oophorectomy a few years before, and had since given birth to a boy.

Initial tests by the GP

- Sperm samples are best produced after two to three days' sexual abstinence, by masturbation, and collected in a wide-mouthed sterile container rather than a condom or plastic bag. Sperm specimens should be examined in the laboratory of the licensed or unlicensed fertility clinic to which the couple are likely to be referred. Sperm analysis should be carried out as soon as possible after production within an hour.[1] Although it is recommended that two semen samples should be tested, it is unclear clinically how useful this is when the first sample is normal. There is considerable variability in reference ranges between different laboratories for sperm counts and quality, and it is important to know the laboratory's normal ranges for your population and to select a laboratory that operates according to WHO recommendations[6] with internal and external quality controls.
- Measure serum progesterone in the mid-luteal phase to indicate ovulation; levels above 16 nmol/l for a minimum of five days or a single value above 30 nmol/l suggest that ovulation has taken place[1] as given in Figure 4.2 (although the guidelines[1] point out that only recovery of an actual egg or a pregnancy are 100% guarantees that ovulation has occurred).
- Ovulation predictor kits that detect luteinising hormone (LH) in the urine are widely available and have generally replaced the use of

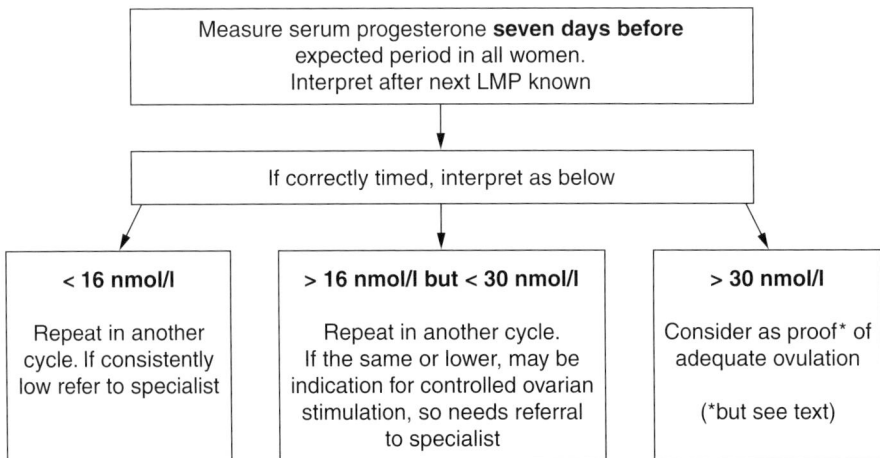

```
┌─────────────────────────────────────────────┐
│  Measure serum progesterone seven days before│
│          expected period in all women.       │
│          Interpret after next LMP known       │
└─────────────────────────────────────────────┘
                        │
                        ▼
┌─────────────────────────────────────────────┐
│       If correctly timed, interpret as below │
└─────────────────────────────────────────────┘
```

< 16 nmol/l	> 16 nmol/l but < 30 nmol/l	> 30 nmol/l
Repeat in another cycle. If consistently low refer to specialist	Repeat in another cycle. If the same or lower, may be indication for controlled ovarian stimulation, so needs referral to specialist	Consider as proof* of adequate ovulation (*but see text)

Figure 4.2: Measurement of serum progesterone. (Reprinted with permission from the Royal College of Obstetricians and Gynaecologists (1998) *Evidence-based Clinical Guidelines No. 2*. RCOG, London.[1])

temperature charts, but the kits are not generally recommended by those working in the field, who feel that couples are best continuing with their normal sexual habit[7] rather than feeling that tests dictate when they must have intercourse.

Box 4.2: Reference values of semen variables[8]

Volume	2.0 ml or more
pH	7.2 or more
Sperm concentration	$\geqslant$ 20 million/ml
Total sperm number	$\geqslant$ 40 million per ejaculate
Motility	$\geqslant$ 50% motile (grades a and b) or $\geqslant$ 25% with progressive motility (grade a) within 60 minutes of ejaculation
Morphology	$\geqslant$ 15% normal forms
Vitality	$\geqslant$ 75% live
White blood cells	< 1 million/ml
Immunobead test	< 50% motile sperm with beads bound
MAR test	< 50% motile sperm with adherent particles

WHO defines a sperm concentration above 20×10^6 per ml seminal fluid as normal, but researchers feel that some men who have sperm counts above this lower limit may also be classed as being subfertile.[9] Assessment of sperm morphology differs between laboratories, so be cautious when interpreting the significance of morphology results. Oligospermia indicates too few sperm, and is often used as an umbrella term that includes sperm with reduced motility or abnormal forms. Azoospermia is the term used to denote the total absence of sperm. Some experts prefer to avoid classifying subfertility in men as anything other than the more general term of a 'male factor' cause, as the sperm contents vary between collections.

References

1 Royal College of Obstetricians and Gynaecologists (1998) *The initial investigation and management of the infertile couple. Evidence-based*

clinical guidelines. No. 2. Royal College of Obstetricians and Gynaecologists, London.

2 Jensen T, Hjollund NH, Henriksen TB *et al.* (1998) Does moderate alcohol consumption affect fertility? Follow up study among couples planning first pregnancy. *BMJ.* **317**: 505–10.

3 Health Education Authority (1996) *Think About Drink . . . there's more to drink than you think.* HEA, London.

4 Souter V, Penney G, Hopton JI and Templeton A (1998) Patient satisfaction with the management of infertility. *Human Reproduction.* **13**: 1831–6.

5 Johnson M and Everitt B (1997) *Essential Reproduction.* Blackwell, Oxford.

6 Royal College of Obstetricians and Gynaecologists (1998) *The management of infertility in secondary care. Evidence-based clinical guidelines. No. 3.* Royal College of Obstetricians and Gynaecologists, London.

7 Hargreave T and Mills J (1998) Investigating and managing infertility in general practice. *BMJ.* **316**: 1438–41.

8 World Health Organization (1999) *WHO Laboratory Manual for the Examination of Human Semen and Sperm Cervical Mucus Interaction* (4e). Cambridge University Press, Cambridge.

9 Bonde JP, Ernst E, Jensen TK *et al.* (1998) Relation between semen quality and fertility: a population-based study of 430 first-pregnancy planners. *Lancet.* **352**: 1172–7.

Reflection exercises

Exercise 5

Review your referral protocol for primary infertility. If you have not got a protocol now's the time to write one or adapt one from the ReproMED website (*see* www.ReproMED.org.uk/book/) or RCOG guidelines.

- Have you updated it?
- Do all the team know and understand the new revisions? Ask them over coffee.

Exercise 6

Undertake a significant event audit around a serious adverse condition that has occurred recently in someone who is being treated for infertility. For instance, a letter about an aspect of the infertility treatment (e.g. an appointment, a test result) being sent to the wrong address or the wrong person. Look at the circumstances leading up to the event. Discuss the case as a team, looking to see if you could have intervened more effectively at any time before the serious complication reached its final state. Could the management have been more effective?

Now that you have completed these interactive reflection exercises transfer the information to the empty template of the personal development plan on pages 122 to 129 if you are working on your own learning plan. Don't forget to keep the evidence of your learning in your personal portfolio.

Part Four: Managing infertility in specialist care

CHAPTER 5

Referring the infertile couple for specialist help

> **Box 5.1:** What to put in the referral letter about the couple
>
> - Patients' personal details – age, contact details
> - Reproductive histories – previous pregnancies, length of time trying to conceive, previous contraception
> - Results of all previous investigations
> - Rubella immunity
> - Any concerns about the welfare of any resulting child

About 70% of couples attending fertility clinics having been referred for fertility treatment eventually achieve a pregnancy, although this may take a long time.[1] Couples who have been attempting to conceive for more than a year require assessment. Couples should be referred early to a specialist clinic if the female partner is aged over 35 years.[2] Other reasons for early referral to a specialist are histories of amenorrhoea, gross menstrual irregularity or significant PID[2] or any patients where the results from the initial investigations were abnormal. Otherwise if the history, examinations and investigations are normal in both partners, referral can be deferred until the couple have been trying to conceive for at least 18 months. However, couples may prefer to be referred early despite this advice, if waiting times to be seen are unduly long and they want to claim their place in the queue.

Patient Box 5.2

'Since we started living together at the beginning of 1997, we had been having unprotected intercourse as I felt sure that I would not become pregnant and I didn't. We approached our GP, who recommended that in the first instance we see a consultant, privately, about whom we had heard great things. I was put on a three-month course of Clomid and underwent hormone tests and follicle tracking during this three-month period. All seemed well. I produced the right level of hormones at the right time of the month and I produced follicles that, it was assumed, would yield ova. Still I did not become pregnant.'

Reasons for referring patients early

Women:

- over 35 years old and trying to conccive for a year
- amenorrhoea or oligo/amenorrhoea
- previous abdominal or pelvic surgery
- history of PID
- history of sexually transmitted disease (STD)
- abnormal pelvic examination
- abnormal investigations.

Men:

- previous or current genital pathology or examination
- previous urogenital surgery
- history of STD
- significant varicocele
- significant systemic illness
- low sperm count/poor sperm quality.

Whenever possible, couples with infertility problems should be referred together to clinics specialising in the management of infertility with easy access to other relevant specialists, such as urologists, rather than the woman being managed in a general gynaecology clinic and her male partner in a urology clinic. Licensed fertility clinics will offer a wider range of treatments than unlicensed centres, backed by well-trained counsellors and appropriate laboratory facilities. There may be factors in both partners which are contributing to their infertile state, and simultaneous investigation and treatment of both is more likely to result in achieving a pregnancy. For instance, a urologist and fertility specialist both need to be involved if the reversal of a vasectomy and ovarian failure are parallel problems, when the freezing and storage of sperm retrieved at the operation may be used in future IVF cycles, and for advanced microsurgical techniques such as ICSI for men with low sperm counts. The only exception where a urology referral might be appropriate in addition to that to a licensed fertility centre is where there are obvious abnormalities of the genitalia.

Choosing the fertility clinic

Fertility clinics have a 'threefold responsibility for:

- the patient's treatment – to get the highest live birth rate they can
- the potential child's welfare – to get the lowest multiple birth rate they can
- the community interest – to get the lowest number of multiple births because of the cost of healthcare for twins and triplets'.[4]

Most of the licensed clinics are in the private sector – it is estimated that only about 20% of fertility treatment is carried out by the NHS. The costs of treatment vary from clinic to clinic; in general the range of costs for IVF and associated drugs varies between £2000 and £3000 per cycle.[5]

The *Infertility Companion*[6] gives information about costs and details of treatment at all licensed clinics at 1996 rates. The HFEA's *Patients' Guide*[7] is available to patients and health professionals free of charge and gives comprehensive information about the treatments available, and outcomes, in each licensed centre. Although the HFEA published a patients' guide in 2002,[8] the following results refer to the guide published in 2000, as the results in the former were brief, provisional and not independently verified by the HFEA. Nevertheless, it is interesting to note that the 2002 guide suggests a slight overall increase in live birth rate following both IVF and DI, but a reduction in the number of patients treated. Live birth rates vary greatly from clinic to clinic, and there is not always an explicit upper age range for treatment. In most clinics the range is between 35 and 50 years, with some clinics specifying different age limits for NHS and private treatment (for example 38 years versus 45 years old for NHS and private treatment respectively, Table 5.1), or for when a woman's own eggs or donated eggs are used in IVF (for example 45 years with own eggs and 50 years with donated eggs).

Table 5.1: Survey of clinic's upper age limits for treating women*

Clinic's upper age limit (years)	Number of clinics
35–40	12
41–45	21
46–50	18
No declared upper age limit	36

*Adapted from Furse.[6]

Box 5.3: Quote from CHILD, the national infertility support network

'It is important that patients understand that they should contact a number of clinics asking the right questions to receive information that is relevant to their own personal circumstances.'

The HFEA's *Patients' Guide*[7] gives details about the number of treatment cycles undertaken in one year, and the outcomes in terms of pregnancy rates, percentage of multiple pregnancies and live birth rates for each licensed clinic. In the past, the media has tended to sensationalise the information about success rates by presenting them as a league table, which may give a misleading impression. Some clinics may appear to have lower success rates than others because they have policies to minimise the risk of multiple births or treat an older age group of women. There are factors other than the live birth rate figures that couples intending to seek treatment should consider if they have a

---

Patient Box 5.4

'We were placed on the waiting list for IVF at our local teaching hospital in April 1998. We were told that the wait would be approximately nine months and we had our first consultation in June 1998, a few months after my 36th birthday. In July 1998, Ian underwent tests to check his sperm. After a lengthy wait we were contacted in April 1999 and asked to attend the Unit for blood tests and for Ian to have his sperm tested again.'

---

choice in selecting their clinic – such as the multiple pregnancy rate, the availability of a full range of fertility treatments and the costs. The *Guide* encourages couples to make an informed choice about the centre they opt for and provides a checklist of criteria, summarised in Box 5.5. The couple's expectations of the clinic may be very high before they embark on treatment. Unrealistic expectations can make disappointments more painful. These should be borne in mind when choosing a clinic.

The waiting time for a consultation and the availability of NHS-funded fertility treatment are also critical factors in selecting the fertility clinic to which the couple are referred by their GP. In most clinics, there is no wait or a waiting time of only a few weeks for private treatment, whereas waiting times to be seen for NHS-funded treatment are quoted as being up to five years.[6]

Box 5.5: Checklist of clinic details according to the HFEA's *Patients' Guide*

- Treatments offered
- How comfortable you feel with the staff and the surroundings
- What information and counselling is offered
- Cost
- Location
- Live birth rate

References

1 Dowers A and Yates R (1998) New developments in infertility. *Pulse*. **4 April**.

2 Hargreave T and Mills J (1998) Investigating and managing infertility in general practice. *BMJ*. **316**: 1438–41.

3 Royal College of Obstetricians and Gynaecologists (1998) *The initial investigation and management of the infertile couple. Evidence-based clinical guidelines. No. 2.* Royal College of Obstetricians and Gynaecologists, London.

4 Lieberman B (1998) *Workshop – multiple pregnancy and policy on number of embryos transferred*. Report of the HFEA Annual Conference 1997. HFEA, London.

5 Hansard (1998) The cost of *in vitro* fertilisation. 6 July, col. 389.

6 Furse A (1997) *Infertility Companion: a user's guide to tests, technologies and therapies.* Thorsons, London.

7 Human Fertilisation and Embryology Authority (2000) *The Patients' Guide to IVF Clinics.* HFEA, London.

8 Human Fertilisation and Embryology Authority (2002) *The Patients' Guide to IVF Clinics.* HFEA, London.

Reflection exercises

Exercise 7

First, ask five consecutive patients whose infertility you are managing to describe their perceived risks of developing complications from investigations and treatment.

Have they got realistic perspectives about those risks? Ask them what they think are their chances of achieving pregnancy? For instance, what do those couples undergoing IVF treatment believe is the likelihood of their conceiving with up to three cycles of treatment?

Exercise 8

How can you demonstrate that you are competent in the role you have in infertility practice, whether you are a GP, practice nurse, specialist infertility nurse or infertility consultant specialist? This might be through mapping out the different areas of your practice and then undertaking associated audits, or organising peer reviews or patient feedback to demonstrate the extent of your competence in all those areas.

Could you expand this exercise and work with a colleague in primary or secondary care, for instance one to whom you refer or discharge patients, to demonstrate each other's competence?

> Now that you have completed these interactive reflection exercises transfer the information to the empty template of the personal development plan on pages 122 to 129 if you are working on your own learning plan. Don't forget to keep the evidence of your learning in your personal portfolio.

CHAPTER 6

Fertility treatments

The most important predictors of successful conception in infertile couples presenting for investigation and treatment is the woman's age, previous pregnancy history and duration of infertility, unless the male partner has azoospermia or extreme oligozoospermia.[1,2]

An overview of fertility treatments

Figure 6.1 describes the sequence of investigation and management once the patient has presented to specialist care.

As far as the woman is concerned

- Are the tubes patent? A laparoscopy is the most reliable way to check that the tubes are patent or identify the cause(s) of a blockage. The information obtained from a hysterosalpingogram is limited to the internal state of the tubes and uterine cavity, whereas a laparoscopy visualises the rest of the pelvis, and therefore any adhesions, endometriosis, ovarian cysts or other pathology. However, an out-patient hysterosalpingogram is a less invasive, cheaper and easier test to perform than a laparoscopy, which requires a general anaesthetic as an inpatient, so is often performed to confirm tubal patency in 'low risk' couples, that is for couples where tubal blockage is not the expected cause of their infertility.[1] Women with risk factors for pelvic or tubal disease, an abnormal pelvic examination or secondary infertility should have a laparoscopy as the primary investigation, as they are more likely to have pelvic pathology that would not be picked up by a hysterosalpingogram.[1] The test of hysterosalpingo-contrast-sonography is being evaluated as a potential technique for screening for tubal patency in the future.
- What is the *Chlamydia* status? *Chlamydia* screening should be carried out at the start of infertility investigations, before uterine

```
┌─────────────────────────────────┐
│   Couple referred with infertility │
│          from GP                │
└─────────────────────────────────┘
                │
                ▼
┌─────────────────────────────────┐
│  Check history and examination or │
│   perform if not already done    │
└─────────────────────────────────┘
                │
                ▼
┌─────────────────────────────────┐
│ Initial investigations as per primary │
│   care protocol if not already done │
└─────────────────────────────────┘
                │
                ▼
┌─────────────────────────────────┐
│  Arrange for tubal patency testing │
│  and consider need for Chlamydia  │
│    antigen screening or antibiotic │
│          prophylaxis              │
└─────────────────────────────────┘
                │
                ▼
┌─────────────────────────────────┐
│  Explain any further investigations │
│  and management plan with written │
│      information as backup        │
└─────────────────────────────────┘
```

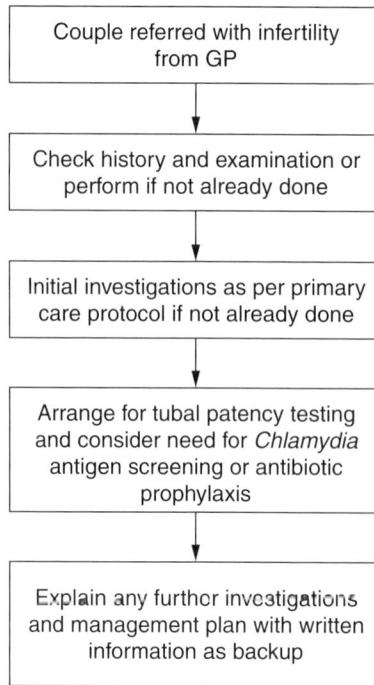

Figure 6.1: The initial investigation and management of the infertile couple in secondary care. (Reprinted with permission from the Royal College of Obstetricians and Gynaecologists (1998) *Evidence-based Clinical Guidelines No. 2*. RCOG, London.[1])

instrumentation is undertaken, to reduce the risk of carrying pre-existent, asymptomatic infection into the upper genital tract from the cervix. *Chlamydia* infection is an important cause of female infertility in that the likelihood of infertility is proportional to the number of episodes of PID the woman has previously suffered; three episodes of PID gives a 50% chance of tubal blockage, which is five times the risk of a single episode of PID.[1] Serology testing may provide evidence of old infection. Doxycycline or azithromycin are the drugs of choice for treating *Chlamydia* infection. *Chlamydia* is also thought to be a cause of male infertility.[1] The sexual partners of people proven to have *Chlamydia* should be traced, notified and treated.

As far as the man is concerned

- Physical examination as above, if it has not already been done.
- Assessment of the sperm – review of the results of the investigations done before referral, or arranging investigations as above if not already undertaken.
- More detailed examination of men whose sperm is abnormal. The endocrine tests FSH and testosterone (and prolactin if there is gynaecomastia) should be undertaken to investigate hypogonadism or help differentiate between an obstructive cause and spermatogenic failure in men with azoospermia or oligozoospermia.[2] In cases of azoospermia or severe oligospermia, chromosome testing is advisable. Imaging with contact thermography, Doppler sonography or angiography are used as alternative investigations for looking at the testes in more depth.[2]

Tests that should only be carried out if they can be justified; not routinely or as a first line

- *An endometrial biopsy.* This has traditionally been used to investigate the response of the endometrium to progesterone and its state of readiness for implantation. A 'luteal phase deficiency' or 'defect' has been thought to indicate that too little progesterone has been secreted by the corpus luteum, but now the reliability of the test and its interpretation are in doubt, and recent guidance is that the luteal phase should not be evaluated by a routine endometrial biopsy, and its usefulness in the investigation of unexplained infertility remains to be evaluated.[1]
- *Postcoital test.* This is a controversial test that is still used in the investigation of infertility. Nevertheless, the test has been shown to provide useful prognostic information for couples with less than three years' infertility, so long as it is properly conducted.[3]
- *Sperm function tests.* A variety of methods of semen analysis have been developed to try and determine particular defects and the severity of the associated male factor infertility. None of the tests seems to be overly helpful in isolation, but experimenting with a combination of tests may give a deeper understanding of the causes of male infertility and more predictive information in future.[1]
- *Sperm antibody testing.* This test is particularly important when assessing men following vasectomy reversal. There are a variety of

tests for screening and quantification of sperm antibodies. Caution should be exercised when interpreting these results – interpretation requires specialist expertise.

- *Hysteroscopy*. As this test involves looking directly at the uterine cavity it can detect uterine abnormalities which are associated with infertility, such as congenital abnormalities, endometrial polyps and submucosal fibroids. However, because there is not yet any evidence that fertility is improved by treating such uterine abnormalities, hysteroscopy cannot be recommended as a routine test for all infertile women.[1]
- *Ultrasound examination of the endometrium*. There is conflicting evidence about the value of ultrasonographic examination of the endometrium for managing infertility and the extent to which the measured endometrial thickness indicates endometrial function or the likelihood of conception. The examination can also be used to assess endometrial texture; this involves a subjective judgement, which may be more meaningful if carried out by a transvaginal as opposed to a transabdominal approach.[1] Such transvaginal imaging gives a more accurate picture of pelvic pathology and may pick up conditions such as polycystic ovaries, which would not be detected by bimanual pelvic examination. The guidelines recommend a transvaginal ultrasound scan of the ovaries in conjunction with a thorough physical examination before assisted conception is started or hormones to induce ovulation are prescribed.[1]
- *Testicular biopsy*. This requires the use of microsurgical skills and specialised equipment by appropriately trained staff. It should not be undertaken as a diagnostic test, as the damage done by the procedure may further reduce the chances of a successful conception in the future. It may be used in specialised centres where there are facilities for recovering sperm to be used immediately for ICSI therapy or for cryostorage (the sperm is frozen and stored for use at a later date).
- *Chromosomal analysis*. Chromosomal analysis should be undertaken in men with sperm counts of less than five or ten million sperm in the ejaculate, because chromosome abnormalities are associated with low sperm counts.
- *Genetic testing for cystic fibrosis*. This is indicated in men with congenital absence of a vas deferens and their female partners.

......Some tests should only be carried out if they can be justified!

Range of fertility treatments

For the infertile woman

- *Tubal surgery*: for patients who are well-selected for likelihood of success, by experienced surgeons trained in microsurgical techniques. Tubal surgery can be as effective as IVF or more so for selected cases of mild distal or proximal tubal obstruction and occlusion. Tubal surgery is unlikely to be successful if both the distal and proximal ends of the tubes are obstructed. IVF might be considered if pregnancy has not resulted within 12 months of tubal surgery that has rendered the tubes patent.[2]
- *Tubal catheterisation*: recommended by the American Fertility Society for patients with proximal tubal obstruction as a minimally invasive alternative to tubal surgery.[2,4]
- *IVF*: should be considered as the first choice of treatment for moderate to severe distal tube disease.[2] Other factors that will influence the decision as to whether or not to embark on IVF are the age of the woman, the relative importance of other infertility factors, and the risks of ovarian hyperstimulation (OHSS) and multiple pregnancy.
- *Reversal of sterilisation by tubal reanastomosis*: operative success rates in women who are still ovulating and have fertile male partners are high, with pregnancy rates described as being in the region of 44–92%.[3] Half of all women aged 40 years and over who have their sterilisation reversed are reported to become pregnant.[2] Surgery should be carried out only in centres with the expertise and facilities to undertake microsurgery.
- *Induction of ovulation*: there are many different reasons for ovarian failure; there may be a genetic cause, an autoimmune disorder, recent weight loss, concurrent drugs or medication suppressing ovarian function, too much exercise, a pituitary tumour causing gonadotrophic deficiency or polycystic ovarian syndrome. The guidelines[2] recommend that investigations to determine the cause and the most appropriate treatment are carried out in a specialist centre with specialist endocrine testing, chromosomal analysis and skilled ultrasonography available. Ovarian induction should only be tried if any male factor subfertility is mild with at least five million sperm per ejaculate, and be limited to six cycles if ovulation occurs but pregnancy does not, before confirming that the fallopian tubes are patent and endometriosis is not a significant problem. The lowest

effective doses of clomiphene and gonadotrophins should be used with careful timing of stimulation at specific points in the cycle to minimise OHSS.[2]

- *Bromocriptine* suppresses prolactin secretion in patients with hyper-prolactinaemia, but the patient may be plagued with side effects such as nausea, vomiting, vertigo and headaches. Cabergoline and quina-golide are more effective and better tolerated than bromocriptine and need to be taken only once or twice weekly.[2] Neither bromocriptine nor danazol are effective treatments for unexplained infertility.

- *Ablation of endometriosis*: results so far suggest that surgical abla-tion of mild or moderate endometriosis improves fertility in sub-fertile women and is more effective than treatment with danazol,[2] which improves the symptoms but not the pregnancy rate. The diagnosis should be proved laparoscopically. IVF or GIFT may be tried if surgery is unsuccessful.[2] IVF has been increasingly employed when previously GIFT would have been used, because of the increased availability of IVF and its improving success rates.

- *Intra-uterine insemination (IUI)* and *ovarian stimulation* is an effective combination for patients with unexplained infertility tried prior to undergoing IVF.[2] Couples need to consider the risks of multiple pregnancy.

Patient Box 6.1

'Naturally, [with Ian] having fathered two children, we thought that this was just a matter of course. The results would be ready after we came back from holiday in the middle of August. When we attended the clinic for the test results we were completely shocked at the news they gave us: (1) Ian's sperm count was very low and the motility exceedingly poor; and (2) we would not be able to have children with conventional IVF but would have to try ICSI. It was a huge blow to us, as this was now the only way in which we could go forward.'

For the infertile man

- *Reversal of vasectomy*: success rates following reversal are quoted as ranging from 17% to over 82%.[2] The chances of success depend on the time since the vasectomy was carried out, the type of the original vasectomy procedure, the existence of other genital pathology and the technical skill of the surgeon attempting the reversal.[2] Successful reversal of vasectomy is not clear cut, and pregnancy rates are only a half or two-thirds of the patency rates of the vas deferens after the reversal operation. For example, patency and pregnancy rates are cited as being 97% and 76% respectively for a reversal operation carried out within three years of the original vasectomy being done.[2]

- *Gonadotrophic drugs*: given for months or years in hypogonadotropic hypogonadism, gonadotrophin drugs can stimulate spermatogenesis and achieve normal sperm counts. Gonadotrophin-releasing hormone is as effective as gonadotrophin drugs but needs to be given by an infusion pump for about a year.[2] Pregnancy may occur before sperm counts reach normal levels.
- *Bromocriptine*: is an effective treatment for men with hyperprolactinaemia and also helps reverse their associated loss of libido and impotence.[3] It is ineffective as an empirical treatment for ozoospermia or poor sperm quality of no known cause, as are anti-oestrogen (such as tamoxifen or clomiphene) and androgen (such as testosterone) drugs, which have been used in the past.[3]
- *Varicocele treatment by ligation or embolisation*: treatment of a man with oligozoospermia appears to improve sperm quality and subsequent fertility, whereas such treatment on an infertile man with normozoospermia has not been found to be beneficial.[2]

Ways of assisting conception

If investigations are normal, but there has been more than three years' infertility, assisted conception should be considered.

Clomiphene

Clomiphene is the most frequently prescribed fertility drug in America.[2] In the UK, it is used by both GPs and hospital specialists as the initial treatment for amenorrhoea or oligomenorrhoea. The guidelines[2] recommend that treatment with clomiphene is tried for women who ovulate with clomiphene and have no other infertility factors, before embarking on more complex or invasive therapy. However, the guidelines[2] highlight the advice from the Committee on Safety of Medicines to limit treatment with clomiphene to six cycles to guard against increasing the treated women's potential risk of ovarian career.

Clomiphene works by increasing the secretion of follicle-stimulating hormone (FSH), which in turn stimulates ovarian follicular development. A course usually starts on the second day of the menstrual cycle and lasts for five days. If the initial dose produces ovulation, the same dose is repeated in subsequent cycles. If ovulation does not occur, the subsequent dose is increased. The lowest effective dose should be used, as one of the side effects is to thicken the cervical mucus, making it more impenetrable to sperm. Clomiphene may be successful in up to 50% of women who are not ovulating properly.[5]

The guidelines stress the importance of ultrasonic monitoring of at least the first cycle where clomiphene is prescribed, to titrate the drug to an appropriate dose and reduce the likelihood of a multiple pregnancy.[2] The risks of multiple pregnancy with clomiphene treatment are reported as being between 2 and 13%.[2] This recommendation will outlaw many GPs from initiating clomiphene treatment, limiting their role to continuing to prescribe and monitor the drug under a shared-care arrangement with a hospital specialist who does have ready access to such ultrasonic monitoring equipment, and is likely to be a contentious issue.

Clomiphene may be used for unexplained infertility that has lasted for a few years, although the benefits are small and the risk of multiple pregnancies should be considered.[6,7]

Recombinant FSH or ovarian diathermy are alternative treatments which may now be tried in women with clomiphene-resistant polycystic ovary symdrome (PCOS).

Metformin

It has been known for some time that PCOS is associated with insulin resistance, particularly if the patient is obese. Insulin-sensitising agents such as metformin have been shown to induce ovulation in anovulatory patients with PCOS, even when they are resistant to treatments such as clomiphene.

Intra-uterine insemination (IUI)

This is the process by which sperm is placed in the woman's uterus by a fine plastic tube, timed to coincide with ovulation. IUI is used for women with patent fallopian tubes. It overcomes barriers to sperm, such as cervical mucus problems where there are high levels of antibodies to sperm, or male fertility problems. It is worth trying in cases of unexplained infertility. The sperm used may be that from the male partner or from an anonymous donor, depending on the nature and quality of the male partner's sperm. If donor sperm is used, the clinic carrying out the procedure must be licensed by the HFEA. If the partner's sperm is frozen rather than freshly produced for the IUI procedure, the storage of that sperm needs a licence too.

Ovulation is timed by monitoring with ultrasonic scans and measuring levels of luteinising hormone (LH) in the urine. Human chorionic gonadotrophin (hCG) may be given by injection to stimulate ovulation by triggering a surge of LH and boost the chances of pregnancy occurring.

Sometimes low doses of the ovarian stimulating hormones clomiphene or gonadotrophins are used in conjunction with IUI. This runs the risk of a multiple pregnancy if more than one egg is released and fertilised, but is sometimes thought to be necessary if a woman has irregular cycles and timing ovulation is difficult. If prior scans show too many eggs have been stimulated, the cycle should be abandoned. The process may be repeated in a subsequent month, or another method such as IVF considered.

The probability of pregnancy with IUI is most likely within the first four attempts, and the likelihood of success is reduced after the ninth attempt. If IUI does not work, patients may move on to try IVF, or ICSI if the infertility is due to a male factor problem.

Donor insemination (DI)

In donor insemination sperm from a donor is introduced via the woman's vagina, through the cervical opening into the cervical canal or into the uterus itself (IUI). The treatment is licensed by the HFEA because it involves insemination with sperm from a donor and not the male partner's own sperm. The donor does not have to be, but usually is, anonymous. It is sometimes carried out in parallel with clomiphene or gonadotrophin therapy to stimulate the woman's ovaries to produce more eggs than usual (stimulated DI). The degree of ovarian stimulation needed is generally far less than for IVF.

The number of DI treatment cycles using donated sperm dropped by over a third in the 1990s, from 25 623 cycles in a 12-month period in 1992/93 to 14 333 cycles in 1996/97.[8] This has mainly been due to the rise in numbers of ICSI treatments being carried out, whereby even men with very low sperm counts can be enabled to achieve a pregnancy with their own sperm. Even azoospermic men are usually suitable for ICSI following surgical sperm retrieval.

DI tends to be used where the man has no or very few sperm, has had a vasectomy and reversal has failed or not been tried, or where the man carries an inherited disease.

Box 6.2: Factors that have a significant effect on the outcome of treatment by donor insemination (DI)

Negative effects
- Age
- Previous DI treatment cycles not resulting in a pregnancy
- Unstimulated treatment cycle (as opposed to stimulated cycle)

Positive effect
- Previous live birth

HFEA figures for success with DI or GIFT using donated gametes to treat 3419 patients give the overall live birth rate per treatment cycle started at UK fertility clinics as 9.6%. Just under half of these patients received parallel treatment with fertility drugs to 'stimulate' the ovaries to produce more eggs.[8] The relative lack of success with DI compared to other assisted conception methods such as IVF or micro-manipulation by ICSI can be seen from the figures given in Table 6.1 on p. 76, which gives comparative information about the live and multiple pregnancy rates for DI, IVF and ICSI techniques. Just over a quarter of patients receiving DI became pregnant with one or more treatment cycles. Multiple births are far more common with stimulated DI compared to unstimulated treatment; two quadruplets, 13 triplets, 68 sets of twins and 635 singleton babies were born after stimulated DI in 1996/97, compared to no triplets or quads, only 15 sets of twins and 896 singleton babies with unstimulated DI.[8]

DI may be requested by lesbian couples or single women. GPs and fertility specialists are advised by defence societies to make a clinically based decision, taking the mother's right to self-determination and the unborn child's rights and welfare into account. The General Medical Council advises doctors not to allow their 'views about patients' lifestyle, culture, beliefs, race, colour, gender, sexuality . . . to prejudice the treatment you provide or arrange'.[9] Catholic, Jewish and Muslim faiths believe artificial insemination by a donor outside marriage to be immoral.

The HF&E Act 1990 prohibits the HFEA from giving out identifying information about donors. The public reportedly want DI to remain anonymous. But a growing number of those using DI feel able to tell their children about the mode of their conception. In one study,[10] one-third of recipients followed up had told their children about their origins, or intended to do so when they were old enough to understand. Two-thirds of those receiving DI had told other people that they had used donor sperm to conceive. Most potential donors of sperm were in favour of the resulting children being told of their origins. Just under half of sperm donors in this study indicated that they would be prepared to be identified to the resulting offspring when they reached adulthood. Allowing people the right to trace their genetic parents is a contentious issue; those who donated sperm, as they thought anonymously, in the past, may be distraught if offspring conceived after donor insemination were able to turn up at their door unexpectedly in the future. It is important that couples wishing to have a further child using the same donor keep in touch with the clinic to ensure that they come back for treatment well before the sperm reaches its length of storage expiry period and by law has to be discarded (usually ten years).

In vitro fertilisation (IVF)

In contrast to the early days of IVF, gonadotrophic injections are given today to stimulate the ovaries to produce more eggs, which has been shown to increase pregnancy rates. The gonadotrophin preparations may be divided into those extracted from postmenopausal urine and those produced using modern recombinant DNA technology. Due to improvements in urinary purification techniques both preparations are of comparable quality and effectiveness but the urinary preparations are less expensive. If gonadotrophin injections were given alone, there would be a high risk of rising oestradiol levels triggering premature release of LH. To reduce the likelihood of this occurring, gonadotrophin-releasing hormone agonists are given either by nasal spray or injection. These block LH secretion, following a few days of treatment, but they are associated with a variety of side effects, including ovarian cyst formation. More recently gonadotrophin-releasing hormone antagonists have been introduced that produce immediate blockage of LH release.

Ovarian stimulation is best monitored using transvaginal ultrasound, and serum oestradiol levels may also be helpful. Sequential monitoring shows when the eggs are ready for collection, and an injection of hCG is given 34–36 hours before recovery. Eggs are usually removed from the ovaries transvaginally under ultrasound direction, using mild sedation. Eggs are mixed with sperm in carefully controlled conditions in the laboratory. The embryos are ready for transfer following two to three days' incubation. In view of concerns about multiple pregnancies, HFEA guidelines state that no more than two embryos should be replaced other than in exceptional circumstances. Any remaining embryos may be frozen for future use. About two-thirds of the frozen

Box 6.3: Factors that have a significant effect on the outcome of IVF treatment

Negative effects
- Older age
- Obesity
- Longer duration of infertility
- Two or more IVF treatment cycles not resulting in a pregnancy
- Presence of a hydrosalpinx
- Poor response to ovarian stimulation

Positive effects
- Previous IVF pregnancy
- Previous live birth
- Younger age

embryos will usually survive the freeze–thaw process and be suitable for replacement in the women's uterus on a future occasion, if the first cycle of IVF using fresh embryos is unsuccessful. The placement of thawed embryos in a woman's uterus can be carried out either in a natural cycle or in a hormonally controlled cycle when gonadatrophin agonists may be used, followed by oestrogen tablets and progesterone vaginal pessaries. As with natural conceptions many pregnancies created by IVF may miscarry.

During a 12-month period in 1996/7, approximately 25 500 patients received IVF treatment in the UK. A total of 33 520 cycles were started, which included frozen embryo replacements, and 27 981 reached the stage at which embryos were transferred. There were 6755 clinical pregnancies created, which led to 5601 births, that is 16.7% of all the treatments started led to live babies.[8] The average live birth rate per treatment cycle of IVF was 15.5% compared to a rate of 21.6% per treatment cycle in which the embryo was created by micromanipulation (mainly the ICSI technique),[8] as Table 6.1 shows. The live birth rate for ICSI is higher than for IVF because the female partner is usually fertile and likely to be younger than those women undergoing IVF.

The age of the woman is the most important factor in predicting success with IVF. The live birth rate for women using their own eggs undergoing IVF is highest for women in the 29–30-year-old age group, at 20.1% per treatment cycle, falling to 2.7% per treatment cycle in women aged 43–44 years old, as Table 6.2 shows.

Women who have been pregnant before are more likely to conceive with IVF than women who have never been pregnant. The live birth

Table 6.1: Live and multiple birth rates for *in vitro* fertilisation, micromanipulation and donor insemination in licensed clinics in the UK during the 12-month period 1996–97*

	Number of treatment cycles	Live birth rate per treatment cycle (%)	Multiple birth rate per live birth event (%)
IVF**	26 868	15.5	26.8
Micromanipulation	6652	21.6	29.1
DI***	14 333	9.6	6.5

*Adapted from data in Human Fertilisation and Embryology Authority's *Annual Report 1998*[8]
**The data for IVF given here do not include cycles involving micromanipulation; they do include transfers with frozen embryos
***The data for DI include GIFT using donor gametes and IUI

Table 6.2: Live birth rate per cycle for women of different age groups undergoing IVF using their own eggs*

	Age of woman (years)				
	Under 27	29–30	35–36	43–44	⩾ 45
Number of cycles	1149	2833	4030	482	202
Live birth rate (%)	18.0	20.1	14.4	2.7	1

*Adapted from data in Human Fertilisation and Embryology Authority's *Annual Report 1998*[8]

rate with IVF is highest for the first cycle, at about 17.4% for fresh embryo transfers compared to a 12.6% live birth rate for the fifth cycle and 8.6% by the eleventh attempt, as shown in Table 6.3. As the number of attempts increases, those who have still not conceived have infertility problems that are more resistant to treatment. About two-fifths of infertile women eventually conceive with a course of IVF involving up to three treatment cycles: the first cycle involves the transfer of fresh embryos and the subsequent two cycles the transfer of thawed, frozen embryos into the woman's uterus. This 40% success rate is termed the cumulative live birth rate. Couples with frozen embryos must keep in touch with the clinic. This will ensure that they are able to renew their consent to storage, extending it when appropriate. They should be encouraged to use their embryos before the storage period expires (usually up to ten years), when, by law, the embryos will have to be discarded.

Table 6.3: Percentage live birth rates per cycle by numbers of attempts for *in vitro* fertilisation, micromanipulation and donor insemination in licensed clinics in the UK during the 12-month period 1996–97*

Number of attempts IVF	1	2	3	4	5	6	7–10	11+
Live birth rate per cycle (%)**	17.4	16.1	16.3	16.5	14.4	12.6	13.8	8.6
Number of attempts Micromanipulation	1	2	3	4	5–8	9+		
Live birth rate per cycle (%)	24.1	21.3	19.2	17.1	18.5	15.0		
Number of attempts DI	1	2	3	4	5	6–8	9–11	12+
Live birth rate per cycle (%)	11.2	10.3	10.5	9.4	8.6	9.4	9.6	7.4

*Adapted from data in Human Fertilisation and Embryology Authority's *Annual Report 1998*[8]
**The data for IVF given here do not include cycles involving micromanipulation; they do include transfers with frozen embryos.

Fresh embryos are more likely to be successful in achieving pregnancies than frozen embryos; the overall live birth for IVF using frozen embryos was only 11.6% per cycle in 1996/97.[8] This is probably because only the exact number of frozen embryos intended to be used are thawed out for transfer in the IVF process and there is no choice about which ones are transferred, whereas in fresh cycles there is often a choice and the best embryos can be selected.

Slightly more boys than girls are born following IVF treatment (51.4% boys compared to 48.6% girls).

Gamete intra-fallopian transfer (GIFT)

The first birth following GIFT took place in 1985. A maximum of three eggs and sperm are surgically transferred into the fallopian tube using the GIFT technique, so that fertilisation occurs in the tube. GIFT is only possible if the female partner has normal patent fallopian tubes and the sperm quality is reasonably good. GIFT is rarely used these days since the availability and success rates of IVF and IUI have improved.

The risk of ectopic pregnancy is around 4%. As with natural conceptions many pregnancies may miscarry.

GIFT does not need to be licensed by the HFEA because fertilisation takes place within the woman's body and the egg and sperm are produced by the couple being treated.

A few clinics use GIFT and IVF in the same treatment cycle, which is a licensable activity. The total number of eggs and embryos transferred cannot exceed three, in the same way that no more than three embryos can be transferred in conventional IVF, in accordance with the HFEA guidelines.

Micromanipulation sperm techniques – usually intra-cytoplasmic sperm injection (ICSI)

ICSI is a relatively new technique and it may be worth re-referring men with very low sperm counts back to a specialist clinic, even if they have been told in the past that they could not be helped. The first birth following ICSI took place in 1992. Since then ICSI has become widely used throughout the world as it enables men to father children of their own rather than use sperm donated by another man.

ICSI is a technique where an individual sperm is injected directly into the cytoplasm of an egg with a fine glass needle, to bypass natural barriers that previously prevented the sperm penetrating the egg. ICSI is used for couples who have failed to achieve successful fertilisation with IVF techniques or where the quality of the sperm is too poor for normal IVF to be likely to succeed. Typical sperm problems are low sperm numbers, poor sperm motility, where there are high levels of anti-sperm antibody, where the vas deferens is absent, where vasectomy reversal has failed or where there is an obstruction in the testis or epididymis to the outflow of sperm. Men with low sperm counts are more likely to have sperm abnormalities, such as microdeletions on the long arm of the Y chromosome. These may be passed on to any sons born as a result of this method of assisted conception, who may in turn have impaired fertility.[2] Although it is recognised that genetic abnormalities may be passed from father to child, evidence to date is reassuring that the ICSI technique itself does not lead to an increased risk of abnormality.

ICSI can use fresh or frozen sperm or a biopsy of tissue from the testis. The surgical retrieval of sperm from the epididymis or testis can be done under a local or a general anaesthetic and takes about 30 minutes. Men can go home after about two hours. The eggs are collected in the same way as for IVF, after stimulating the woman with ovarian hormones. Sperm are injected into several healthy and mature-looking eggs. The injected eggs are observed *in vitro* for 48 hours to check that fertilisation has occurred, whereupon up to three embryos are transferred to the woman's uterus. Spare embryos can be frozen for future use, which makes repeating the exercise easier and cheaper because there is no need to collect eggs and sperm first.

Patient Box 6.4

'After two or three samples were given, they told us that they had frozen one batch, had approximately 18 straws and that we would use this batch of sperm for our ICSI cycle. We commenced our first treatment cycle.

We had been given a lot of information about the treatment cycle, but because one cannot truly understand the mechanics until you have done it, we had not appreciated that at each step, we had to face a giant hurdle. First, I had to sniff a substance twice in the morning and twice in the evening, at roughly the same times so as to bring down my hormone levels to baseline or, in the words of the Unit, to down regulate. It takes an average of three weeks to get to the point where your hormones are at the correct level before proceeding to the next stage. Down regulating really means that you become post-menopausal. I had hot flushes morning, noon and night, bad skin, mood swings and generally felt not myself, really rather grotty.

Once you are at this point, you then progress to the second stage, which is stimulating the ovaries or rather, over-stimulating them, by injecting quite large amounts of oestrogen, so as to produce as many follicles as is safely possible in the hope that the follicles will yield good and healthy eggs. This proved to be a nerve-wracking time. I am needle phobic and so the thought of having to inject oestrogen daily for two weeks, quite apart from the many blood tests that you have to endure to check hormone levels, made me panic. A few years earlier I had discovered a topical anaesthetic called Emla cream and so I asked the Unit for several tubes and a specific type of plaster, similar in appearance to clingfilm and which holds the cream firm to the spot that you want to numb, and they willingly gave me a supply. Ian was brilliant at injecting and so with the Emla cream we managed very well. I also used the cream for the regular blood tests and this made a huge difference to how I approached the whole process.

continued

When you have been stimulated sufficiently and the follicles are at a certain size and maturity, you are ready to move on to the third stage, egg retrieval. The first time I did it, I had it done without general anaesthetic and that proved to be extremely painful. However, they managed to get enough eggs, six in total, and they took them away to be fertilised. You are told that the embryologist will call you at home the next morning at, say, 10am, to let you know if any of the eggs have fertilised and if so how many and how they are looking. When the telephone rang the next morning, I really didn't want to answer it, as I was scared of what I might be told. On this occasion it was good news, three had fertilised and were graded as "A" grade – top grade. I was 37 years old and as it was my first attempt at this, we were advised to transfer back a maximum of two embryos and so we did. Then comes the hardest time of all, the two-week wait . . .

The wait between embryo transfer and the pregnancy test feels like an eternity. We were advised not to have sexual intercourse; I was advised not to swim and to shower as opposed to taking baths. I was also told that I should not put my life on hold but to carry on as usual but not to be too strenuous about housework, carrying heavy shopping and the like. As it happened, we were moving house the day after my embryo transfer and although I didn't heft things around it was, nevertheless, a very stressful time.

The second cycle never got to embryo transfer stage as they didn't manage to get any of the very few eggs – two! – to embryo stage. We were absolutely crushed by this. We immediately made an appointment to see one of the senior doctors and when we saw the doctor I asked the question that had been burning in my mind: had I run out of eggs? Was I becoming menopausal?'

An increasing number of fertility clinics are offering ICSI. The HFEA's *Patients' Guide*[11] lists 56 of the 103 licensed fertility clinics as offering it. A total of 5828 patients were treated by micromanipulation in 1996/97 and 6652 cycles of treatment were provided by licensed fertility clinics in the UK. Ten terminations, 229 miscarriages, 18 ectopic pregnancies and 1896 live babies resulted. Most of these were using the ICSI technique, but there were a few using other similar techniques, which have mainly been discontinued.

The overall live birth rate per treatment cycle for micromanipulation in UK fertility clinics was 21.6% in 1996/97.[8] Pregnancy rates are around 30–35% per cycle for sperm obtained from the ejaculate of semen or directly from the epididymis, and about 20% when carried out using testicular sperm.[12] As with IVF, women in the 29–30-year-old age group have the best chance of becoming pregnant, with 28.1% live birth rates per cycle of treatment compared with a 3.1% chance of a live birth per cycle in women over 45 years old.

For audit purposes, replacement of embryos produced following IVF at the same time as those resulting from ICSI, is discouraged. Fertility centres must record how often such a process occurs.

Spermatids

These are immature precursors of spermatozoa. They carry the same genetic information as sperm but have not yet finished maturing. Their use is confined to research purposes in the UK, and the HFEA has not issued any clinics with a licence to use spermatids in treatment. There is debate about the potential of using round spermatids, which are very immature, as opposed to the more mature, elongated spermatids, in treating patients. It is thought that spermatids may be useful for fertility treatment in the future in men in whom it proves impossible to retrieve mature sperm for use in ICSI. There is concern about the difficulty of distinguishing between a spermatid and an immature spermatozoon from the testis that has still to complete spermatogenesis and journey through the epididymis,[13] and that spermatids may inadvertently be used in some micromanipulation treatment processes.

The HFEA will consider whether to license spermatids for treatment once there is sufficient evidence about the safety and efficacy of the use of spermatids in ICSI. Such evidence will be accumulated from animal studies and human embryo research. Spermatids are used to treat infertility in some overseas fertility centres by their direct injection into eggs using the ICSI technique. Success rates in creating pregnancies have so far been very low.

References

1 Royal College of Obstetricians and Gynaecologists (1998) *The initial investigation and management of the infertile couple. Evidence-based clinical guidelines. No. 2.* Royal College of Obstetricians and Gynaecologists, London.

2 Royal College of Obstetricians and Gynaecologists (1998) *The management of infertility in secondary care. Evidence-based clinical guidelines. No. 3.* Royal College of Obstetricians and Gynaecologists, London.

3 Glazener CM, Ford W and Hull M (2000) The prognostic power of the post-coital test for natural conception depends on duration of infertility. *Human Reproduction.* **15**(9): 1953–7.

4 American Fertility Society (1993) *Guideline for Practice. Tubal disease.* American Fertility Society, Birmingham, Alabama.

5 Dowers A and Yates R (1998) New developments in infertility. *Pulse.* **4 April**.

6 Rossing M, Daling J, Weiss NJ *et al.* (1994) Ovarian tumours in a cohort of infertile women. *New Eng J Med.* **331**(12): 771–6.

7 Hughes E, Collins J and Gandekerikhove P (2000) Clomiphene citrate for unexplained infertility in women. *Cochrane Database Syst Rev.* **3**: CD000057.

8 Human Fertilisation and Embryology Authority (1998) *Annual Report 1998.* HFEA, London.

9 General Medical Council (2001) *Good Medical Practice.* GMC, London.

10 Shepherd ST (1998) *Donor Insemination. Payment, anonymity, secrecy and disclosure.* Infertility Research Trust, Jessop Hospital, Sheffield.

11 Human Fertilisation and Embryology Authority (1998) *Interim Patients' Guide.* HFEA, London.

12 Ndukwe G (1997) New treatment for male infertility. *GP News.* **7 November**.

13 Lewis S and McClure N (1998) Difficulties in distinguishing between a mature spermatid and a testicular spermatozoon. *Human Reproduction.* **13**: 2979 (letter).

Reflection exercises

Exercise 9

Having read through the material in this chapter do you have a good understanding about the range of fertility treatments? Or do you need to read and study more? You could look up the original references cited here or consult our ReproMED websites for details of courses and other sources of help (*see* www.ReproMED.org.uk/book/).

Exercise 10

Look out all the patient literature you have for patients and couples with infertility problems. Does the literature match the most up-to-date thinking about best practice? Has all your literature been written and produced within the last three years? Or does the literature promote out-of-date practices and approaches, or use old terminology? You need to be clear what the most up-to-date recommendations are yourself to be able to check your literature and complete this exercise.

Now that you have completed these interactive reflection exercises transfer the information to the empty template of the personal development plan on pages 122 to 129 if you are working on your own learning plan. Don't forget to keep the evidence of your learning in your personal portfolio.

CHAPTER 7

Risks of fertility treatments

Multiple pregnancy

Multiple pregnancy is a common outcome from using fertility drugs because the ovaries are stimulated to produce several eggs at a time, or more than one embryo is transferred to the uterus in IVF, or more than one egg is replaced in GIFT. Two-thirds of triplets and higher order pregnancies are due to ovarian induction with clomiphene and gonado-trophin drugs.[1]

Clinics balance the risk of multiple pregnancy against gaining an acceptable pregnancy rate. The number of embryos that can be trans-ferred after IVF is limited to two (three in exceptional circumstances) by the HFEA, and of course there is a further chance that a single embryo could subdivide to give an identical set of twins or triplets. Respected authorities[2–5] are pushing for a policy whereby a maximum of two embryos are transferred when more than three have been created. Three embryos were intentionally replaced in more than half of the cycles of IVF carried out in the UK in 1995/96. This approach led to the high overall multiple birth rate in the UK. Forty-seven per cent of individual babies born from all types of IVF came from a multiple pregnancy in 1996/97.[6] This compares with a spontaneous conception rate of less than one multiple pregnancy in a hundred in couples not receiving any infertility treatment.

Reducing the multiple pregnancy rate will require a substantial change in professional practice and patient outlook. Table 7.1 shows the comparative miscarriage and stillbirth/neonatal death rates for single and multiple pregnancies resulting from IVF, with more than four times as many twins and more than ten times the numbers of triplets compared to single births.[6] Most multiple pregnancies are delivered before full term and about one-third of twins will be delivered pre-term before 37 weeks' gestation. The average length of pregnancy for triplets is 34 weeks and that for quadruplets is 32.5 weeks.

Table 7.1: Single and multiple clinical pregnancy outcomes after IVF or frozen embryo transfers in the 12-month period 1996–97[*]

Number of babies	Outcome of pregnancy		
	Live births	Miscarriages	Stillbirth and neonatal deaths (per 1000 births)
Singleton	3867	674	9.6
Twin	1502	218	44.6
Triplet	230	59	87.0
Quadruplet	2	–	500.0

[*]Adapted from HFEA *Annual Report 1998*[6]

Premature babies are more likely to be of low birth weight. The average birth weight of a single baby is 3.3 kg, compared to 2.5 kg for twins and 1.8 kg for triplets. Babies born very prematurely are more likely to have a disability such as cerebral palsy; 38% of infant survivors born at 24 weeks and 24% of survivors born at 26 weeks are handicapped.[7] Maternal obstetric complications are more likely in multiple pregnancies than in women bearing singleton babies. The majority of triplets and quadruplets are delivered by Caesarean section.

Even though most patients know and seem to understand the risks of multiple pregnancy, many still choose to have three embryos replaced. The prospect of twins or triplets can seem attractive to infertile couples who are desperate to conceive. They think that a multiple birth will save them from having to repeat the fertility treatment procedures to become pregnant again in the future, saving them hassle and money. Such couples need to be well informed about the serious risks and consequences of multiple births. New parents can find multiple births far more of a strain than they had anticipated – financially, practically and emotionally – and may even regret having the much longed-for babies. Women who had hoped to return to work may find that the childcare costs are far more than for one baby and make it difficult financially for both parents to return to work.

Clinics give patients different advice on the number of embryos that should be transferred. Some base that advice on the woman's age. If she is over 40 years old they recommend the transfer of three rather than two embryos as she is less likely to become pregnant. However, the evidence is that there is as much chance of a live birth if the best two of four or more fertilised eggs available for transfer are replaced than if three embryos are replaced in a woman's uterus.[5] Replacing a maximum of two embryos reduces the chances of a multiple birth[5] and makes the creation of triplets unlikely. Today, three embryos can only be replaced in exceptional circumstances. Table 7.2 illustrates the success rates where at least four embryos are available for transfer.

Fetal reduction may be carried out as a planned procedure to terminate the life of one or more fetuses in a multiple pregnancy. The procedure is usually carried out between 11 and 12 weeks' gestation. Usually the operative reduction is carried out so that two fetuses remain, both of which have an improved chance of developing normally into healthy babies; and the mother is less likely to have obstetric complications. A particular fetus might be selected for termination if it appears to be weaker than the others, or alternatively the fetus to be sacrificed may be picked at random. The risks from fetal reduction have to be carefully balanced: carrying out embryo reduction on triplets to achieve twins can increase the probability of the pregnancy being carried to more than 32 weeks' gestation, but also increases the risks of miscarriage, with a 15–17% risk resulting form the procedure.[4] The decision to opt for fetal reduction is a very difficult emotional dilemma for parents, who will require much time and support before and after the operation.

Table 7.2: Pregnancy rates and multiple pregnancy rates in relation to age of woman and number of embryos transferred, where at least 4 embryos had been available for transfer (Centre for Reproductive Medicine, Bristol, 1 January 1997–31 December 2000)

	2 embryos transferred			3 embryos transferred		
	Pregnancy rate % (†)	Twins %	Triplets %	Pregnancy rate % (†)	Twins %	Triplets %
< 35 years	33.4 (n = 311)	25	2.9	31.7 (n = 432)	35	13.9
35–39 years	25.5 (n = 94)	12.5	0	29.9 (n = 347)	31.7	4.8
⩾ 40 years	25 (n = 12)	67	0	15 (n = 113)	17.6	0

† Total in parenthesis

Ovarian hyperstimulation syndrome (OHSS)

The condition occurs in about 4% of women receiving ovarian stimulating drugs,[8] and is severe in 0.5–2% of all IVF cycles.[8] Its occurrence is not predictable, and all women undergoing ovarian stimulation with hormones should be warned of the signs and symptoms of OHSS and have emergency contact numbers to hand for obtaining immediate advice and help from the specialist fertility centre.

Cases may present with lower abdominal discomfort or pain, abdominal swelling, nausea and later vomiting, and in more severe conditions ascites, pleural effusion and venous thrombosis requiring hospitalisation. The ovarian stimulating treatment should be immediately discontinued and any fertilised eggs frozen for use on another occasion.

The risk of OHSS is reduced by close monitoring of the number and size of the developing follicles during ovulation induction cycles by measuring the serum oestrogen and ultrasound scanning. OHSS only occurs following the ovulatory injection of hCG. Thus cancellation of ovarian stimulation prior to this point may avoid the complication.

Medical complications

One report describing the incidence of complications arising during 3500 treatment cycles in couples undergoing conventional IVF or ICSI, using either ejaculated or surgically retrieved sperm,[9] gave the overall medical complication rate from assisted reproduction techniques as 8.3%. OHSS occurred[9] in a moderate form in 6% and in a severe form in 2% of cycles. Other complications were relatively uncommon: vaginal bleeding in three patients, deep vein thrombosis in four, hemiparesis in two patients, an acute abdomen that necessitated laparotomy in three patients (two for ruptured heterotropic pregnancies and one for torsion of an adnexal cyst) and anaesthetic complications in two patients.[9] Four men had testicular infections following 575 surgical retrievals of sperm. The one patient who died due to liver failure following OHSS had withheld information about her previous liver damage from hepatitis C from the clinicians treating her.

The emotional rollercoaster of fertility treatment

The state of infertility is very difficult for many couples to come to terms with. Typically, the couple decide it is time to start their family and stop using contraception. The woman confidently expects to become pregnant almost straight away, having spent the last few years trying hard to remember to use contraception and not take any chances with unprotected intercourse and pregnancy. After the first few periods arrive, perhaps with one or two false hopes if they start a little later than expected, she and her partner become progressively more despondent and very emotional at the first sign of menstrual loss. Men may tend to assume that the blame for the couple's infertility is more likely to lie with the female partner, especially if they associate infertility with being less 'manly'. If the woman has had a previous termination she could well be feeling very guilty about her past, especially if she has not told her partner about the termination(s).

The couple will have invested a lot of emotion in their first visit to the GP to discuss the delay in their conceiving. It may be the first time they have talked publicly about their problem. They may be disappointed to realise that there will be no instant solution to their delay in conceiving and that they are expected to wait longer for spontaneous conception to occur. Then they may become progressively more frustrated by waiting for test results at the practice, or maybe a long wait to be seen by an NHS specialist at a fertility clinic.

The infertile couple need as much reliable information as possible at this stage. They need to be able to understand their situation, assess their options and discard the myths about the causes and circumstances of infertility that others may tell them. If the couple are not well informed they might press for treatment that is inappropriate, such as a quicker referral to a urology or gynaecology clinic rather than wait to be seen at a fertility clinic.

Those who undergo the sequence of specialised fertility investigations and assisted conception treatments describe the emotional rollercoaster of the highs and lows in the different stages of their treatment. Their expectations may be fuelled by embarking on new treatments only to be dashed when eggs and sperm fail to fertilise, or treatment has to be abandoned because of complications, or when a miscarriage, or worse still a stillbirth, occurs. The quotes from some infertile couples surveyed[10] describe some of these feelings (*see* Box 7.1).

Box 7.1: Selection of comments by men and women who responded to the National Infertility Awareness Campaign's survey[10]

'The strongest feeling was one of total and utter failure.'

'Our relationship has experienced extremes of despair and then strength. Only we understand, like other infertile couples, the pain.'

'Infertility not only had a marked effect on my relationship with my partner but also with friends, family and complete strangers. The pressure to be "normal" in today's society is extreme and the lack of government support via funding and inadequate diagnosis makes infertility an abnormality.'

'The area of infertility is a very traumatic one – filled with obstacles and difficulties that you can never imagine when you first start out.'

'. . . there was no support for people in our situation in this area, in fact there is an overwhelming feeling of hitting a brick wall as we cannot afford private treatment.'

The many intertwined emotional and ethical decisions taken by infertile couples in the course of treatment can be distressing. Being involved in weighing the balance between achieving a successful pregnancy and the risks of creating a multiple pregnancy is one of the most fundamental dilemmas. It is asking a lot for an infertile couple to make a rational decision when they are longing for a baby and do not fully appreciate the increased chances of abnormalities and complications from multiple pregnancies, nor the financial, practical and emotional hardships of caring for twins, triplets or more babies.

The potential risk of ovarian cancer

Those women who are infertile already have an increased risk of ovarian cancer. It is known that pregnancy protects against ovarian cancer and involuntary childlessness increases the risk of ovarian cancer. Because the evidence suggests that clomiphene is associated with an increased risk of ovarian cancer if used for 12 cycles or more, a cautious approach is to restrict clomiphene to no more than six cycles. The balance of evidence to date does not suggest that gonadotrophin therapy increases the lifetime risk of ovarian cancer. Until more is known from the ongoing follow-up trials, all infertility drugs should be used at the lowest effective doses possible, to minimise any potential risks of ovarian cancer.

References

1 Levene MI, Wild J and Steer P (1992) Higher multiple births and the modern management of infertility in Britain. *British Journal of Obstetrics and Gynaecology.* **99**: 607–13.

2 Coetsier T and Dhont M (1998) Avoiding multiple pregnancies in *in-vitro* fertilisation; who's afraid of single embryo transfer? *Human Reproduction.* **13**(10): 2663–4.

3 Lieberman B (1998) An embryo too many? *Human Reproduction.* **13**(10): 2664–6.

4 Murdoch A (1998) How many embryos should be transferred? *Human Reproduction.* **13**(10): 2666–70.

5 Templeton A and Morris J (1998) Reducing the risk of multiple births by transfer of two embryos after *in vitro* fertilisation. *NEJM.* **339**(9): 537–7.

6 Human Fertilisation and Embryology Authority (1998) *Annual Report 1998.* HFEA, London.

7 Rennie J (1996) Perinatal management at the lower margin of viability. *Archives of Diseases in Childhood.* **74**: 214–18.

8 Royal College of Obstetricians and Gynaecologists (1998) *The management of infertility in secondary care. Evidence-based clinical guidelines. No. 3.* Royal College of Obstetricians and Gynaecologists, London.

9 Serour G, Aboulghar M, Mansour R *et al.* (1998) Complications of medically assisted conception in 3,500 cycles. *Fertility and Sterility.* **70**(4): 638–42.

10 Braude P and Ledger W (1998) *Infertility into the Millennium.* National Infertility Awareness Campaign, London.

11 Royal College of Obstetricians and Gynaecologists (1998) *The initial investigation and management of the infertile couple. Evidence-based clinical guidelines. No. 2.* Royal College of Obstetricians and Gynaecologists, London.

Reflection exercises

Exercise 11

Undertake an analysis of the strengths, weaknesses, opportunities and threats (SWOT) of the way your practice or unit operates its systems and procedures for managing people with infertility. This will entail convening a group to represent all elements of your team (for instance, GP, nurse, manager/support staff, hospital specialist, infertility counsellor). You will be considering:

- your infrastructure – capacity for computerised recall, management protocols, access and availability of fertility clinics, hardware and software, information resources
- your capability – staff numbers and posts, skills (clinical skills such as more advanced levels of infertility care; personal and communication skills; IT)
- your capacity – how you cope with demand
- the extent to which you work as a team across the practice, with others from secondary care or the independent sector, and most of all with patients – including responding to feedback to achieve patient-centred care.

Use the 14 components of clinical governance described in Chapter 1 as a checklist for the SWOT analysis, then make a plan for improvements – what you need to learn (and transfer your needs and action plan to your personal development plan), what you need to buy, who you need to appoint or involve and what you need to reorganise.

Exercise 12

Arrange for the local infertility specialist to visit a local general practice for an in-house educational session. Discuss referral letters written to the hospital and the recent letters from consultant to the practice. Could you have done more in primary care? Were the responding letters from the hospital staff appropriate – do they need to learn more about the problems of general practice? Review the referral protocol and discuss how to provide more seamless care for patients, shifting work and resources to primary care as far as possible.

Invite the local community pharmacists, the infertility counsellor and the fertility nurses to join you for this educational session and encourage them to contribute to the discussions.

Now that you have completed these interactive reflection exercises transfer the information to the empty template of the personal development plan on pages 122 to 129 if you are working on your own learning plan. Don't forget to keep the evidence of your learning in your personal portfolio.

Part Five:
The wider aspects of fertility treatment

CHAPTER 8

The wider aspects of fertility treatment

Cryopreservation therapy

Cryopreservation is the freezing of oocytes, sperm or embryos and their storage in liquid nitrogen for thawing and transfer at a later date. The process is now available in most clinics. The use of frozen human eggs is still experimental as there is insufficient information about safety; research is continuing in this field. The HFEA requires specific licences for centres using frozen eggs for treatment. Some embryos do not survive being frozen, but the suggestion that abnormal embryos are more likely to be killed by freezing has yet to be proven.

Sperm donors are screened for HIV, hepatitis B and C, cytomegalovirus and syphilis. The gametes are stored for 180 days and a second HIV antibody test is undertaken to exclude the possibility that the male donor was infected with HIV but had not yet developed antibodies in his blood. The HFEA recommend screening for HIV, hepatitis B and C for people wishing to store gametes and embryos for their own use, such as people about to undergo oncology or radiotherapy treatment, or a woman suffering from OHSS who wishes to freeze her embryos for future use.

Pregnancy rates with frozen as opposed to fresh embryos are lower (12% of 4908 transfers of frozen embryos resulted in live births as opposed to 18% of fresh embryo transfer for 23153 patients treated by IVF[1]). There does not appear to be an increased risk of miscarriage or congenital abnormality, and the cryopreservation process does not appear to adversely affect the growth or health of children during infancy and early childhood, although more follow-up studies are needed to be sure.[2] There is no increase in obstetric or perinatal complications in pregnancies resulting from the transfer of frozen embryos, nor is there any evidence of genetic damage to embryos according to research studies on animals.[3]

There has been no recorded incident in the UK of cross-contamination with stored gametes and embryos intended for treatment, such as from microbial or viral infection. The good laboratory practices that licensed clinics have established minimise such risks.

The media have reported that a couple were exploring the possibility of storing their frozen embryos to allow them to time conceiving their children at convenient stages in their lives. The 32-year-old would-be mother apparently wanted to delay motherhood until she was 40 years old and reduce the chances of infertility or congenital abnormalities occurring then.[4] Such an arrangement would be legal so long as the length of storage was less than the maximum statutory period, which can be extended up to ten years. However, the assisted conception techniques involved in creating the embryo and transferring it to the prospective mother's receptive uterus is invasive and expensive, and less likely to succeed than natural conception. The story has provoked a new ethical debate over the relative justification of freezing embryos for social reasons as opposed to medical reasons, and why if frozen embryos are stored for an infertile couple it is wrong not to extrapolate that facility to fertile couples too. If the couple later split up, the embryos could not be used without both partners' agreement.

The removal and storage of testicular or ovarian tissue

Testicular or ovarian tissue containing gametes can only be stored on licensed premises with the patient's written consent; pre-pubertal tissue that does not contain gametes can be stored on unlicensed premises. If immature gametes are taken from the tissue and matured *in vitro*, then the HF&E Act applies and subsequent storage, treatment or research with those gametes must be licensed and the appropriate consent obtained.

Anyone who has attained the age of 16 years and is of sound mind may give legal consent to surgical or medical treatment or procedures. The issues for children under the age of 16 years are discussed later in the book in the section on 'Consent' (*see* page 108).

The maximum statutory storage period for embryos was extended in 1996 from five to ten years. In some cases consent can be renewed and storage can continue until an individual partner is 55 years of age. Once the permitted storage period has expired, the embryos must be allowed to perish.

Little is known about the long-term effects of prolonged storage on frozen embryos, but there is said to be no evidence that the length of storage will increase the incidence of abnormalities in frozen embryos later used for creating pregnancies.

Donation of gametes

There is a legal limit of ten pregnancies per male or female donor because of public unease. The upper age limit for sperm donors is 55 years old, whereas that for egg donors is 35 years old. The restrictions on age and number apply to donated sperm or eggs, not those recovered from either partner for their own use. The HFEA makes exceptions where a couple want to have another child using the same donor who provided gametes used in conceiving a previous child.

Gametes can be imported from overseas to a specific licensed clinic under a special direction by the HFEA, who will require satisfactory information about the sender, whether the donor gave consent to the export of the gametes, the purpose of the import, reassurance that the donor was appropriately screened and the nature of material being imported. There is a problem where gametes originate from overseas in that some overseas centres will not provide the names of donors because of preserving confidentiality about their identity. Treating centres in the UK have to rely on the overseas centre's assurances that consent has been properly obtained from the person donating the gametes or whose gametes were used to bring about the creation of the embryo in question.

Embryos can only be exported overseas with the written consent of the provider of those gametes under a special direction from the HFEA, and similar information as for the import of gametes or embryos.

Anonymity

The HF&E Act (1990) makes it an offence for licensed clinics or the HFEA to disclose the identity of donors. The only exception where the HFEA may disclose identifying information is if a child that was born with a disability as a result of the donor's failure to disclose an inherited disease were to sue a clinic for damages. If this were to occur, a court might require the HFEA to disclose the donor's identity under the Congenital Disabilities (Civil Liabilities) Act 1976. Whether individuals have a right to know their genetic background continues to be a matter of public debate. The Department of Health is looking at this issue at the present time, so there is a possibility that those conceived from donor eggs or sperm could trace their genetic parents in the future, but a change in primary legislation would be required, and the strength of public feeling on the topic makes it unlikely that any such change in the law would be applied retrospectively.[5]

Paternity

The birth mother is the legal mother of any child born from licensed assisted conception treatments. Thus an egg donor does not have any legal rights over, or responsibilities for, any child resulting from treatment with her eggs. Similarly, a sperm donor is not the legal father of any child who results from treatment with his sperm. The resulting child's birth certificate will not have any indication that either a sperm or egg donor was involved in the conception. Where a single woman is treated with donor sperm, there will be no entry under the section for 'father' on the birth certificate.

Payments to donors and 'egg sharing' in IVF

Egg and sperm donors can receive payments of up to £15. The HFEA would prefer that sperm and eggs were donated as a voluntary gift and are looking for ways to promote a culture of altruism.

Egg donors have to undergo extensive medical screening, and then be primed with hormones to stimulate their ovaries to produce plenty of eggs. This means that they are subject to the side effects of powerful hormones before having an operation under general anaesthetic to retrieve the eggs through the vagina, after which they need time to convalesce. Some clinics encourage women needing egg donation to find and recruit egg donors to donate to them, or anonymously to other women, in return for which the clinic will expedite their IVF treatment.

Some women going through IVF may choose to share surplus eggs with someone else, but usually they agree to this arrangement in return for free or subsidised IVF treatment. All treatment should be preceded by a clear contract which is termed in favour of the donor. As donated eggs are in short supply, this arrangement allows women who have no eggs but who can afford to pay for private treatment to receive IVF, and those who are unable or unwilling to pay for private treatment to receive IVF. Eggs can be shared disproportionately between the donor and recipient so that the donor retains more, to balance the donor's chances of conceiving from a particular batch of eggs. Otherwise, the woman donating eggs in this way is less likely than the woman receiving her eggs to become pregnant, because of the differing reasons for the causes of their infertility in the first place. It is the egg donor who takes most of the risks of treatment from the ovarian stimulation, and if a woman gives away a proportion of her eggs rather than going on to freeze embryos for her own future use, she will have to repeat the ovarian stimulation procedures if she does not become pregnant and wants to try IVF again. The HFEA introduced specific guidelines to regulate egg sharing in the fifth edition of its Code of Practice,[6] following a public consultation exercise which supported the continuation of egg sharing as an option.

It seems that few women who have donated eggs in return for IVF treatment have regrets about sharing their eggs with another infertile woman.[7,8] They seem to have been genuinely glad to have helped other women like themselves to become pregnant using their eggs, and if they failed to become pregnant themselves and their egg sharers did, seem pleased that their efforts were not in vain. One study concluded[8] that 'as long as egg donation is not covered by the NHS, it is fairer to offer egg sharing than to refuse treatment to those unable to pay'.

> **Box 8.1**
>
> 'Egg sharing is a loving anonymous donation in just the same way as altruistic egg donation. Some would say more so, because it is a gift from one woman who has suffered the pain of infertility to another who has gone through a similar experience.'[9]

The more that independent counsellors and GPs are involved in discussions with potential egg or sperm donors, and can explain the ethical and practical implications of donation, the better informed such donors can be about their choices.

The welfare of the potential child created by donated gametes should be of paramount concern, but even the welfare of the child is regarded in alternative ways by those for and against banning payments to donors and used to justify their arguments and platforms. On the one hand, supporters of banning payments think the resulting children might have their sense of self-worth undermined if they believe that their birth parents had purchased their genes, while those who support egg sharing or the reimbursement of 'reasonable expenses' argue that the children might be grateful to their birth parents for taking such trouble to procreate them.

Pre-implantation genetic diagnosis

Pre-implantation genetic diagnosis (PGD) is a technique used to detect inherited genetic disorders in embryos before they are transferred to the uterus. There are two types of PGD: tests for particular disorders and tests for a sex-linked disorder. This entails the removal of one or two cells from an embryo for genetic analysis, usually at two to three days after fertilisation when the embryo consists of 8–16 cells. Studying two cells rather than one gives a better picture and more chance that the material is representative of the whole embryo as cells vary considerably; it is not possible to take more than two cells for analysis at this stage. In this way, affected embryos may be identified and only healthy embryos without the genetic defect transferred as part of an IVF procedure. Such early diagnosis will avoid termination in mid-pregnancy if prenatal diagnosis detects a genetic defect. Prenatal testing is carried out by chorionic villus sampling or amniocentesis, with an associated 1–2% risk of subsequent miscarriage.

A few hospitals have been licensed to offer PGD for specific disorders – the X-linked Duchenne disease, cystic fibrosis, Tay Sachs, spinal muscular atrophy, β-thalassaemia and Huntington's chorea. Following a public consultation exercise in 1993, the HFEA decided that sex selection by PGD should not be used for social reasons but be confined to identifying sex-linked disorders with 'serious or life-threatening diseases and disorders' such as the reduced life expectancy or quality of life of affected individuals. The HFEA is working with the recently constituted Advisory Committee on Genetic Testing to develop licensing parameters for PGD in the future.

Reports do filter through of experiments in sex selection occurring abroad;[10] the particular method cited has triggered concerns about the potential risks of sperm being stained with dye and exposed to ultraviolet light to aid separation of X and Y chromosomes. The procedure exploits the size difference between X and Y chromosomes by sorting sperm through the disproportionate uptake of fluorescent dye by X-bearing sperm containing more DNA than Y-bearing sperm. X and Y sperm are then sorted to increase the chances of achieving a baby of the desired gender through IVF or IUI procedures. However, the process is imprecise and only capable of sorting sperm up to about 85% of

X-bearing sperm and 65% of Y-bearing sperm, compared to the usual 50–50 mixture of untreated sperm.

Counselling

Patients should be as well informed as possible about the ethical and practical implications of treatment and should know all the details of the range and success of different methods of assisted conception. Easy access to an independent infertility counsellor is an important option for those undergoing investigation and treatment. Patients may want to discuss whether and when they should embark on alternative treatments or stop treatment with someone with another perspective than that of the treating team away from the clinic setting.

Proper counselling is quite rightly an important requirement of the legislation controlling all assisted conception treatments in the UK. It is mandatory in the UK that these counselling options are available to all patients, although patients may choose to decline counselling they feel inappropriate. There are three main types of counselling, explained below.

Implications counselling

Implications counselling means giving accurate, understandable, factual information to enable infertile couples to make their own confident decisions about how to proceed. This is usually included in the consultation with the doctor when outlining treatment options and discussing treatment choices. However, there is often too much information to take in, thus it is helpful to reinforce this with written information, and discussions between the patients and other members of the fertility team, particularly the nurses, both before and during treatment (*see* Box 8.2).

Patient Box 8.2

'We had been given a lot of information about the treatment cycle but because you cannot truly understand the mechanics until you have done it, we had not appreciated at each step we had to face a giant hurdle.'

Support counselling

Support counselling refers to the emotional support that infertile couples often need, particularly when experiencing the stress that a course of treatment can bring (*see* Box 8.3). Any members of the specialist team can provide the support, and it is an important reason why all members of the team should have a basic understanding of counselling and clear guidance on how to refer patients for therapeutic counselling if required.

Patient Box 8.3

'When the two-week wait was up, I took in a sample of urine for my pregnancy test that had been booked at the Unit on the day of my embryo transfer. Somehow I just knew it hadn't worked. I wasn't surprised when our nurse returned and told us that I was not pregnant. Ian was very composed although his face changed colour dramatically and he became very red faced. I felt dreadful and for some reason it felt like it was happening to someone else. The only way for me to hang on to my composure was to immediately book in for a second cycle three months later. We were devastated, but really kept this to ourselves, thinking that if we just ploughed on we would be fine. So many emotions are invested in taking part in a treatment cycle and it is very difficult to explain to others exactly how awful you feel when it doesn't work.'

Therapeutic counselling

Therapeutic counselling is help given by someone who is not directly concerned with the actual treatment to enable patients to explore their feelings and give balanced consideration to their lives as a whole. Some couples need to be saved from their own unrealistic and overwhelming pursuit of fertility, and to be helped to come to terms with remaining childless. In the Centre for Reproductive Medicine Bristol, one in five couples attend at least one independent therapeutic counselling session. Although many couples are sceptical of the value of counselling before the session, most couples find these sessions highly beneficial (*see* Box 8.4).

Patient Box 8.4

'The third cycle went as smoothly as is possible . . . My period started the evening before I was due to go for my pregnancy test. Ian was away at a conference and wasn't due back until the following evening. In the morning, I called the Unit, who asked me to come in anyway and to bring my sample as it was possible that I may have retained one or two of the three embryos and so could be pregnant, or I could even have an ectopic pregnancy. Before I could go to the Unit with my sample, I had to take my stepdaughters to school. I found it extremely difficult to pretend all was well in front of the girls, who are not aware that we have been undergoing this treatment. I really just wanted to scream and howl.

 While I waited for the results of the pregnancy test, I babbled on to my nurse about nothing in particular. I felt desperate beyond belief. It was at this juncture that it became apparent to her and to me that I needed to talk to someone. The Unit employs counsellors to be available at the Unit for two days a week and as it happened, I was very lucky as it was one of those days and one could see me immediately. I spent two hours pouring out all my worries, frustrations and problems. I felt immense relief afterwards and much, much stronger.'

Counsellors should also be able to help infertile couples decide when to cease treatment and come to terms with their continued childlessness, which really comes under the umbrella of bereavement counselling. Local and national patient support groups also offer practical and emotional support.

 Infertility counsellors often come from nursing, social work or psychology backgrounds. The British Infertility Counselling Association and British Fertility Society accredit infertility counselling qualifications. Those with the Diploma in infertility counselling will know about the causes of subfertility and sterility, the type and reason for various medical investigations, and have an in-depth knowledge of alternative treatments and the drugs used. They will be aware of the physical, psychological and social effects of infertility treatment, the issues surrounding the welfare of any future children, and the roles and responsibilities of other health professionals involved in delivering fertility care. Training as an accredited counsellor involves practical supervision by another qualified counsellor, to ensure that the new counsellor can apply their theoretical knowledge in the clinical setting.

There are many ethical and legal considerations in reproductive healthcare, for the donor, the recipient, the partner, existing and potential children. As techniques become more sophisticated and new developments make conceptions possible in specific circumstances for the first time, counsellors have to keep abreast of new ethical dilemmas as they unfold.

Each licensed fertility centre should offer couples the opportunity to see a well-qualified counsellor who is independent of the centre, as well as making counselling available from staff at the centre. Such an independent counsellor may reassure the consulting infertile couple that there are no commercial considerations involved in the advice they are given about treatment options.

A new area where counselling is needed is when genetic testing on donated gametes reveals a genetic defect of which the donor was previously unaware. Pre-test information and counselling must be offered, with subsequent advice and support for those donors who turn out to be carriers. The couple need to be informed and counselled of the risks where such screening has not been done; and to receive reliable and comprehensive information about the meaning and the limitations of screening when it is carried out.

Ethics committees

It is not obligatory for licensed fertility clinics to have ethics committees, but is accepted good practice. Most, but not all, clinics have ethics committees that advise the clinic on ethical matters of policy or issues relating to the provision of assisted conception. Members do not consider specialist medical matters in the way that district medical ethics committees consider general health-related research submissions. Their remit is wide, and they consider and advise on such issues as the ethnic factors that affect ethical decisions about fertility treatment and the appropriateness of treating unconventional couples such as lesbians, and should act as a check on 'over-enthusiastic social engineering'.

Genetic testing

Genetic disorders affect about 1% of the population at birth. Genetic testing detects the presence of, or a change in, a particular gene. Genetic disorders may be recessive or dominant. In an autosomal recessive disorder such as cystic fibrosis or sickle cell disease, a defective gene has to be inherited from both parents, and a person carrying one gene (a heterozygote) is usually unaffected by the disorder. Only males are affected by X-linked recessive genetic disorders such as Duchenne muscular dystrophy, and all daughters of affected males are carriers. In an autosomal dominant disorder, such as Huntington's chorea or polycystic kidney disease, inheriting one defective gene from one parent is sufficient for the person to be affected by the disorder. Those with an autosomal dominant condition have a one in two chance of passing it on to their children. Genetic test results need to be interpreted in the light of medical and family histories, and genetic counselling should be seen as a complex specialism as there are so many multifactorial disorders.

Cystic fibrosis is the commonest genetic disorder among the Caucasian population in the UK whereby a recessive disorder involving a single gene can cause serious disease. About one in 25 healthy adults carry the effective gene; one in 2500 children are affected by cystic fibrosis when they inherit two defective genes, one from each parent.

Genetic testing can diagnose people who are suffering symptoms of a condition or detect people who will develop a particular disorder later in life, or are carriers of a disease. Genetic tests for susceptibility to diseases such as cancer, heart disease and diabetes have been developed. Testing is undertaken using blood or urine samples or cells from inside the mouth.

Fertility clinics should take 'all reasonable steps to prevent transmission of a serious genetic disorder . . . Genetic testing should be limited to the determination of carrier status for inherited recessive disorders'.[6] Although screening for cystic fibrosis is not mandatory, it is strongly recommended;[6] specific diseases mentioned for which egg and sperm donors should be screened are cystic fibrosis, and Tay-Sachs, β-thalassaemia and sickle cell anaemia where appropriate for specific population groups.

All those donating gametes should be screened for HIV and other sexual diseases, and common genetic diseases such as cystic fibrosis, but it is not feasible to screen everyone who is being treated with their own eggs or sperm for everything. The HFEA recommend clinics screen all patients for HIV, hepatitis B and C before cryopreserving their gametes to reduce the chances of cross-contamination, although with good laboratory practices this should not be an issue. Many clinics screen men undergoing ICSI too, because in general, poor sperm quality is associated with an increased incidence of sex chromosome abnormalities.

Issues of consent

Informed consent involves knowing about:[11]

- the nature and purpose of the intervention
- the intended effects and unintended side effects
- the risks, harms and hoped-for benefits
- any reasonable alternatives.

No licensed treatment should be given to any person without their written consent to all the stages of the particular treatment. The only exception would be in a case where someone's life was at risk if emergency treatment was not given and he or she was incapable of giving consent, as for any other life-threatening condition.

Consent to treatment or storage should be informed and voluntary. There should be no coercion, fraud or constraint applied to any person giving consent in a healthcare context. The consenting person has a right to refuse or withdraw from the situation without prejudicing their future healthcare. The person has a right to ask questions and to negotiate aspects of their treatment.[12] People giving consent to the use to which their gametes or embryos may be put or how they will be stored, may vary or withdraw their consent at any time before the gametes or embryos are used.[6] Gametes must not be taken from anyone who is not capable of giving valid consent.

The long-term partner or spouse of a person receiving or donating gametes does not have to consent to the treatment or donation of eggs or sperm for treating infertile couples,[6] but it is good practice to encourage any such partner to give their written consent too and it may avoid legal disputes about paternity in the future if the couple are unmarried. A woman's husband will be the legal father of a child born after treatment with donated sperm unless they are legally separated or there is evidence that he did not consent to treatment. Where the couple are unmarried when the treatment is carried out, the male partner will acquire 'legal paternity' of the child who is born provided that:

- the couple received treatment together
- the male partner consented to the treatment.

However, there is a legal distinction between 'parental responsibility' and 'legal paternity', and 'parental responsibility' is not automatically granted to unmarried men who become fathers as a result of receiving treatment with their partner at a licensed fertility clinic. Unmarried couples who may be affected should seek advice from a legal adviser about their own circumstances.

Any donor of eggs or sperm must give written consent about the specific use for which the gametes are intended, which might be for the treatment of themselves, for themselves and a named partner, to provide treatment for others or for research. People must give consent to the gametes being stored, stating what should be done with the gametes or embryos if they die or become incapable of varying or revoking their consent. Several instances of sperm donation from a braindead patient and the use of stored sperm after men have died has provoked public debate about the ethics and morality of creating children whose fathers died a considerable time before they were conceived. Posthumous storage or use of sperm or eggs without effect-ive consent is unlawful in the UK in all cases. Ideally anyone intending to donate organs or tissues after their death should have their written consent witnessed by others.

The law does not specify at what age a child is considered old enough to give consent. A child who understands what the medical treatment is, its purpose, why it is proposed and any risks, and the consequences of not receiving the proposed treatment, can consent to treatment. He or she is regarded as being 'Gillick competent', following the 'Fraser' guidance that emerged in the case.[13] The judge in this case instructed that a child under the age of 16 years would have the capacity to consent to prescribed contraception if she was of sufficient maturity to understand the nature and consequences of that consent. The kind of situation in which consent to treatment by under-16-year-olds becomes important is where they are about to undergo chemotherapy which may threaten their fertility and storage of gonadal tissue for possible later treatment might be considered. It is currently unclear whether treat-ment using gonadal tissue may ever be possible, but sperm from post-pubertal boys may be cryopreserved. While parents can consent to a child's examination and treatment, the child's consent is needed for storage of their gametes if they have reached puberty. This is really 'staged consent' – a 14-year-old may be able to give consent to store his gametes but not allow their use to achieve a pregnancy. If later he wished to use his sperm to have a child, he could give his consent for treatment. However, in the eventuality of his death, his parents would not be able to use the sperm to achieve a pregnancy, even if they were able to find a suitable female.

Surrogacy

Surrogacy describes the arrangement by which a woman acting as a surrogate mother 'agrees to bear a child for another woman or a couple (the intended parents) and surrender it at birth'.[14] Surrogacy should be arranged only where it is medically impossible or undesirable for a woman to carry a child, such as after a hysterectomy, and not for purely social reasons, such as avoiding pregnancy disrupting a woman's career. However, such good practice is not enforceable as it is possible for surrogacy to be carried on a do-it-yourself basis where health professionals are not involved.

In partial surrogacy, the child is genetically linked to the surrogate mother and the male of the commissioning couple (the intending parents) by the prospective father's sperm being placed in the surrogate mother's vagina and fertilising the surrogate mother's egg. This may be performed by self-insemination at home, away from any health service clinic, or by a health professional in a licensed fertility clinic. In full surrogacy, the resulting child has no genetic link with the surrogate mother and the embryo is usually created from the eggs and sperm of one or both of the commissioning couple using the IVF technique. If one or both of the intending parents are unable to produce eggs or sperm themselves, donated sperm or eggs can be used in the IVF procedure. About 60 couples per year use IVF surrogacy.[15]

Surrogacy is not illegal, but the commissioning couple cannot legally force the surrogate mother to give them the child once it is born. Trouble may arise if the child is born with a disability or the commissioning couple change their minds about being parents for any other reason, or if the surrogate mother decides to keep the child once it is born. The HF&E Act (1990) states that 'no surrogacy arrangement is enforceable by or against any persons making it'. When the child is born the surrogate mother is the legal parent. So long as one of the intending parents is genetically linked to the child and the surrogate mother consents, the commissioning couple can apply for a parental order within six months of the birth of the child; otherwise they have to follow formal adoption procedures. If the surrogate mother has a partner, he is the legal father of the resulting child even though the sperm of the intending father was used to create the embryo. Surrogacy can be arranged by individuals or agencies provided they are not profit making; surrogate mothers can be paid expenses by the commissioning couple, but not wages to reward their time or effort.

Surrogacy obviously has many emotional risks for the commissioning couple, the surrogate mother and her partner, not to mention the physical risks to the surrogate mother if the intending father is not screened for sexual diseases in a do-it-yourself arrangement, or there are problems in pregnancy. There are also implications for the siblings and other relatives of the child, who may grieve for the baby being taken away after birth to live with the commissioning couple.

Surrogacy regulations are being tightened up to prevent women acting as professional surrogates and taking up surrogacy as an alternative to paid employment outside the home. Reports have priced women 'renting out their womb' at up to £15 000 per baby.[16] If loss of earnings is taken into account when reimbursing expenses, such a sum might easily be justifiable.

Cloning

Cloning is not envisaged as ever being permitted as a method of artificial human reproduction of whole human beings, but this section is included in the book for information about its potential for developing new treatments and furthering knowledge through research on ageing, cancer, infertility, congenital disease and miscarriage.

Cloning is performed by either artificially dividing a single embryo into two parts to produce identical twins, or by nuclear replacement where foreign genetic material is introduced into the cytoplasm of an unfertilised egg or embryo whose own genetic material has been previously removed. An entire animal is produced from a single cell in 'reproductive cloning', in the same way that Dolly the sheep was created by the nuclear replacement of an egg.[17] Dolly was generated by transferring the nucleus of an udder cell taken from a six-year-old sheep into an unfertilised egg which had its own nucleus removed. Since then, other scientists in America have proved that cloning Dolly was not a fluke as they have managed to clone several generations of mice. Animal reproductive cloning research is aimed at improving the genetic make-up of livestock.

Reproductive cloning is the creation of a fetus, baby or adult who is genetically identical to another fetus, baby or adult, whether alive or dead.[18] The HFEA bans any research which has human reproductive cloning as its aim.

Therapeutic or non-reproductive cloning is any use of a cloning technique undertaken for medical purposes, 'which does not result in the production of genetically identical fetuses or babies'.[18] The term 'cell nucleus replacement' has been coined to describe the process of cloning. The process involves removing the genes from an egg with a fine needle. Stem cells are extracted from the tissue to be cloned and fused with the empty egg using an electric current. Researchers expect that using cloned tissue in this way to repair damaged tissue will avoid rejection of transplanted tissue. Possible examples cited as benefiting from developments in therapeutic cloning might be the cultivation of brain cells to replace cells damaged by Alzheimer's or Parkinson's diseases.

A person's identity is not only determined by their genetic make-up, as environmental and social influences also affect an individual's development – which means it is impossible to produce an exact replica of a person by cloning. Some of the grave concerns about cloning include the reasons why the cloning of a particular person should be wanted in the first place – such as the desire to replace a loved person who has died. A child resulting from such an origin would be unlikely to be allowed to function in their own right, and would be unfairly expected to replicate their predecessor's behaviour and feelings.

There is a great deal of public disquiet about the growth of the biotechnological industry and developments in cloning techniques. The distinction between the research and developments allowed under the umbrella of therapeutic cloning and the disallowing of any stages in reproductive cloning will need to be made explicit.[17,18]

Research involving human embryos

All research studies need to be licensed by the HFEA and gain approval by the researchers' own local ethics committees. Spare, unwanted embryos generated by treatment may be used for research purposes with the parents' written consent. Research is limited to the first 14 days of an embryo's life after fertilisation has occurred.

The purpose of any research on embryos must be confined to promoting advances in the treatment of infertility, increasing knowledge about the causes of congenital disease or miscarriages, developing more effective techniques of contraception or detecting the presence of gene or chromosome abnormalities in embryos.[10]

References

1 Human Fertilisation and Embryology Authority (2000) *Patients' Guide*. HFEA, London.

2 Wennerholm, UB, Albertsson-Wikland K and Berg C (1998) Post-natal growth and health in children born after cryopreservation as embryos. *Lancet*. **351**: 1085–90.

3 Wood MJ (1997) Embryo freezing: is it safe? *Human Reproduction*. **12** (national supplement): 32–7.

4 Brennan Z (1998) Woman freezes embryo for sake of her career. *Sunday Times*. **16 August**.

5 Human Fertilisation and Embryology Authority (1998) *Update, August 1998*. HFEA, London.

6 Human Fertilisation and Embryology Authority (2001) *Code of Practice 2001*. HFEA, London.

7 Ahuja K, Simons E, Fiamanya W *et al.* (1996) Egg-sharing in assisted

conception: ethical and practical considerations. *Human Reproduction.* **11**(5): 1126–31.

8 Ahuja K, Mostyn B and Simons E (1997) Egg sharing and egg donation: attitudes of British egg donors and recipients. *Human Reproduction.* **12**(12): 2845–52.

9 Ballantyne A (1998) Watchdog may end women's shared hope. *The Times.* **23 November**.

10 Bendall K (1998) Sex aid for conception control. *Financial Times.* **21 November**.

11 World Medical Association (1989) Declaration of Helsinki. In: *World Medical Association Handbook of Declarations.* Ferney Voltaire, World Medical Association.

12 Alderson P and Goodey C (1998) Theories of consent. *BMJ.* **317**: 1313–15.

13 Gillick versus West Norfolk and Wisbech Area Health Authority (1985) **3** *All ER*: 402.

14 British Medical Association (1996) *Changing Conceptions of Motherhood. The practice of surrogacy in Britain.* BMA, London.

15 Department of Health (1998) *Surrogacy Review.* The Stationery Office, London.

16 Murray I (1998) Rent-a-womb surrogates face ban. *The Times.* **15 October** (editorial).

17 Wellcome Trust (1998) *Public Perspectives on Human Cloning.* Wellcome Trust, London.

18 Human Genetics Advisory Commission and Human Fertilisation and Embryology Authority (1998) *Cloning Issues in Reproduction, Science and Medicine.* HFEA, London.

Reflection exercise

Exercise 13

Find out what initiatives have been undertaken by any of the team to ascertain patients' views in the previous 12 months. How was the information gained from the initiative used? Did changes result? Your own or team members' learning needs from this exercise might include the following.

- Learning more about the variety of methods that can be employed to find out patients' views.
- Learning how to apply any of these methods to find out the views of

people with infertility about the care or services provided, or that they wish to receive.

- Learning more about organising a survey so that the findings are useful in making changes to the way services are planned or delivered, or staff behave.
- Learning more about involving individual patients in decision making about the management of their infertility.

Now that you have completed this interactive reflection exercise transfer the information to the empty template of the personal development plan on pages 122 to 129 if you are working on your own learning plan. Don't forget to keep the evidence of your learning in your personal portfolio.

CHAPTER 9

The costs and availability of fertility treatment

The availability, accessibility and range of NHS-funded fertility treatments provided varies greatly from region to region. The varying selection criteria set by different health authorities means that often, the availability of NHS-funded fertility treatment depends more on geographical location (known popularly as the 'postcode lottery') and social situation than patients' needs. Such selection criteria include: the woman's age, whether or not either one of the infertile couple have had a previous child, the length of the couple's stable relationship or whether the woman has been previously sterilised. Waiting lists are long even if couples fulfil the selection criteria.

ICSI is more expensive than conventional IVF. Retrieving the sperm surgically is an additional cost. The relative costs of different treatments given by one clinic[1] are:

Conventional IVF per cycle	£2255
ICSI per cycle	£2995
ICSI with surgical retrieval of sperm per cycle	£3935
Initial consultation and investigations	£290
Ovarian stimulation drugs per cycle	£500–1000

In addition, there are the hidden costs of IVF associated with multiple pregnancies and pre-term deliveries.

Rationing and eligibility for fertility treatment

IVF was one of the first treatments to be explicitly rationed by the NHS. In 1993, the purchasing plans of six of 114 health authorities in the UK explicitly stated that they would not be buying any IVF or GIFT treatments for their populations. At the other end of the scale, some other authorities were investing heavily in purchasing more services for their localities.[2] The differences in outlook were based on diverse interpretations of the relative importance of factors considered in assessing the needs of their local populations. The presence of local champions, whether there was a local provider, and pressure from local GPs and the community appeared to be important influences on whether health authorities purchased fertility services.

Local public health experts in different health authorities interpreted the evidence about cost-effectiveness and assessed needs differently, for example whether infertility could be categorised as a health need. There were rough and ready assessments of the relative health gains of different treatments, and authorities started devising qualifying criteria about how to allocate limited treatment resources. Some started querying whether there should be equity of access in the NHS across the UK, and if so, whether there should be a national decision about how to ration fertility treatment on a fair basis.

Since the early 1990s, the geographical variation in the availability of NHS-funded treatment has become more marked. There has been a rapid increase in the level of IVF treatment funded by the NHS overall, but an increasing division between health authorities willing to fund high levels of treatment and those funding no treatment at all.[3] The criteria health authorities are using to define eligibility for NHS treatment and limit access vary greatly. Some authorities limit funding for assisted conception but do not restrict funds for tubal surgery, which may mean that patients with severe tubal damage will be referred for tubal surgery if this is their only option, even though assisted conception is the most appropriate treatment. A survey of all health authorities and boards in the UK in 1997 found that, on average, they were purchasing about one-third of the number of IVF cycles per population of that recommended for the provision of a comprehensive subfertility service.[3,4]

Patient Box 9.1

'I feel strongly that there should be nationally agreed funding criteria, so that all patients are treated fairly . . . the lottery patients currently face depends on their postcode, and whether the GP is sympathetic and willing to prescribe drugs for them, which is completely unjust.'[5]

Only 6% of responding health authorities or boards do not use eligibility criteria when deciding to fund IVF. Ninety-nine per cent put limits on the woman's age, 30% on the man's age, 94% on the number of previous children, 49% on the length of the couple's relationship and 67% on the number of previous cycles of assisted conception. Eighty-eight per cent of health authorities or boards limited the number of treatment cycles they were prepared to fund.[3] The maximum age limit for infertile women seeking IVF ranged from 34 years (3% of health authorities or boards) to 43 years (1%), with the median age being 38 years. One-quarter of health authorities or boards who purchased assisted conception did not fund the drugs. There was a variation in waiting time for assisted conception treatment from up to a year after referral (14 authorities) to more than four years after referral (three authorities).

Patient Box 9.2

'I must point out that, at that time, our local health authority in the area in which we live funded three cycles of IVF treatment for people under the age of 39. Our third cycle would be our last free cycle and so if this didn't work we knew we would have to try to find the £3000 per cycle to carry on.'

The National Infertility Awareness Campaign's call[5] for national guidelines should ensure that: 'eligibility criteria are based on clinical need, that the most appropriate treatment is given to an individual couple and that decisions to treat are based on the potential for a successful outcome'.

References

1 Jenkins J and Corrigan L (2001) Charge Sheet from Centre for Reproductive Medicine, Bristol.

2 Redmayne S and Klein R (1993) Rationing in practice: the case of *in vitro* fertilisation. *BMJ*. **306**: 1521–4.

3 College of Health (1997) *Report of the fifth national survey of the funding and provision of infertility services 1997*. National Infertility Awareness Campaign, PO Box 206, London W1A 3DZ.

4 *Effective Health Care Bulletin* (1992) The management of subfertility. **1**(3). NHS Centre for Reviews and Dissemination, University of York.

5 Braude P and Ledger W (1998) *Infertility into the Millennium.* National Infertility Awareness Campaign, London.

CHAPTER 10

Draw up and apply your personal development plan

Although you will probably want to focus on the investigation and clinical management of infertility in your personal development plan (PDP), you may also wish to include personal management skills, such as your IT capability. As we explained in the Introduction to the book, you may decide to allocate 50% of the time you intend to spend drawing up and applying a PDP in any one year on learning more about infertility practice.

The four worked examples of PDPs that follow are comprehensive, and you may not want to include so much detail in your own PDP. You might include different topics and educational activities – because your needs and circumstances will be different from those of the example practitioner here.

Transfer the information about your learning needs from any of the reflection exercises at the end of the chapters that are relevant to you, and that you have completed, to the empty template of the PDP on pages 122 to 129. The reflection exercises you select will depend on the particular focus of your personal development plan – as in the worked examples here.

The conclusions you have made at the end of each exercise will feature in the action plan of your PDP. Some ideas about other preliminary information you should be gathering for your PDP are given in the boxes of the template.

Template for your personal development plan

Photocopy the following pages and complete your own.

What topic have you chosen?

Who chose it?

Why is the topic a priority?

   (i)   A personal or professional priority?

  (ii)   A practice or department priority?

(iii)   A district priority?

(iv)   A national priority?

Who will be included in your personal development plan?
(Anyone other than you? GPs/medical colleagues, nursing staff, others from outside the practice or unit, patients?)

How will you identify your learning needs?
(How will you obtain this information and who will do it: self-completion checklists, discussion, appraisal, audit, patient feedback? Include details about baseline performance.)

What are the learning needs of the practice or unit and how do they match your needs?

Is there any patient or public input to your personal development plan?

Aims of your personal development plan arising from the preliminary data-gathering exercise:

How might you integrate the 14 components of clinical governance into your personal development plan focusing on the topic of . . . . ?

Establishing a learning culture:

Managing resources and services:

Establishing a research and development culture:

Reliable and accurate data:

Evidence-based practice and policy:

Confidentiality:

Health gain:

Coherent team:

Audit and evaluation:

Meaningful involvement of patients and the public:

Health promotion:

Risk management:

Accountability and performance:

Core requirements:

Action plan
(Include objectives, timetabled action and expected outcomes.)

How does your personal development plan tie in with other strategic plans?
(e.g. the practice's or unit's business or development plan)

What additional resources will you require to execute your plan and from where do you hope to obtain them?
(Will you have to pay any course fees? Will you be able to organise any protected time for learning in working hours?)

How will you evaluate your personal development plan?

How will you know when you have achieved your objectives?
(How will you measure success?)

How will you disseminate the learning from your plan to the rest of the practice team and patients? How will you sustain your newfound knowledge or skills?

How will you handle new learning requirements as they crop up?

Check whether the topic you have chosen to learn about is a priority and the way in which you plan to learn about it is appropriate.

> **Your topic:**

How have you identified your learning need(s)?

(a) PCO or hospital requirement ☐   (e) Appraisal need ☐

(b) Practice or unit business plan ☐   (f) New to post ☐

(c) Legal mandatory requirement ☐   (g) Individual decision ☐

(d) Job requirement ☐   (h) Patient feedback ☐

(i) Other ☐

Have you discussed or planned your learning needs with anyone else?

Yes ☐   No ☐   If yes, who?

. . . .

What are your learning need(s) and/or objective(s) in terms of:

Knowledge. What new information do you hope to gain to help you do this?

. . . .

Skills. What should you be able to do differently as a result of undertaking this learning in your development plan?

. . . .

Behaviour/professional practice. How will this impact on the way you then do things?

. . . .

Details and date of desired development activity:

. . . .

Details of any previous training and/or experience you have in this area/ dates:

. . . .

What is your current performance in this area compared with the requirements of your job?

Need significant development ☐   Need some development ☐
in this area   in this area

Satisfactory in this area ☐   Do well in this area ☐

What level of job relevance does this area have to your role and responsibilities?

Has no relevance to job ☐   Has some relevance ☐

Relevant to job ☐   Very relevant ☐

Essential to job ☐

Describe how the proposed education/training is relevant to your job:

. . . .

Do you need additional support in identifying a suitable development activity?

Yes ☐   No ☐

What do you need?

. . . .

Describe the differences or improvements for you, your practice, PCO and/or hospital trust as a result of undertaking this activity:

. . . .

Assess the priority of your proposed educational/training activity:

Urgent ☐   High ☐   Medium ☐ Low ☐

Describe how the proposed activity will meet your learning needs rather than any other type of course or training on the topic:
. . . .

If you have a free choice would you want to learn this? Yes/No

If no, why not? (please circle all that apply)

It is a waste of time
I have already done it
It is not relevant to my work, career goals
Other

If yes, what reasons are most important to you? (put in rank order)

To improve my performance
To increase my knowledge
To get promotion
I am just interested in it
To be better than my colleagues
To do a more interesting job
To be more confident
Because it will help me

Record of your learning activities

Write in the topic, date, time spent, type of learning, etc. for each activity

	Activity 1	*Activity 2*	*Activity 3*	*Activity 4*
In-house formal learning				
External courses				
Informal and personal				
Qualifications and/or experience gained				

Worked example 1. Personal development plan for a GP or nurse working in primary care focusing on learning about infertility practice in general

Who chose the topic?

It might be your own choice or the practice team may have chosen it because they think someone should lead on infertility matters.

Why is the topic a priority?

(i) A personal or professional priority? You may have seen a need for it yourself or as an inevitable development in your work. You may have agreed as part of your work development, or as a requirement of a change in work duties or responsibilities.

(ii) A practice priority? You may have volunteered after a significant or adverse event highlighted the need for improvement.

(iii) A district or national priority? The primary care organisation may need additional expertise in infertility practice, to represent or advise other practice teams.

Who will be included in your personal development plan?

You might like to find others in your team who want to increase their skills. Working together or as a cascade of learning from each other makes learning more cost-effective. You might include the following:

- GP colleagues
- practice nurse
- community midwife (might be interested in some aspects)
- community pharmacist
- member of patients' support group.

How will you identify your learning needs?

You will probably delegate data collection from audits of practice to designated support staff or the practice manager. You might gather some baseline information as a team, e.g. running a SWOT analysis. For example:

- Strengths and Weaknesses: enthusiasm; willingness to learn – strong educational ethos in the practice; good communication skills and inter-professional relationships to enable inter-disciplinary working; user-friendly and well-designed software and hardware in the practice, for keeping good records.
- Opportunities: an in-practice expert; local training courses run by fertility centre.
- Threats: deficiencies in equipment, software or availability of training; other commitments; antagonism or lack of support from others.

What are the learning needs of the practice and how do they match your needs?

A prioritising exercise as part of drawing up the PDP should have already given you some information. Consider inviting people to make suggestions about the learning and improvements they perceive are needed at a practice team meeting.

You might want to learn more about counselling in general and fertility problems in particular. This wider knowledge might benefit the practice work as a whole.

Is there any patient or public input to your plan?

If you are intending to change your services, what do your patients think about it? Do you know what they think about privacy in the consulting room – can patients be overheard by others waiting outside? Do they want to see their medical records more readily? Do they have concerns about who will access the information and the level of confidentiality? Are there confidentiality issues that concern patients – about getting test results for example?

Do patients want to be involved in designing information on health matters? Do they want you to have a website? How do you manage general public enquiries to a practice website? Do patients want the development of electronic transmission of prescriptions to the pharmacist of their choice? Do they want to email their prescription requests to you? Would patient-held electronic medical records be acceptable?

What mechanism(s) will you use to find out the answers in a meaningful way – not just from the most opinionated or compliant? You may need to think deeply about the reliability of any method, and how representative individual patients are of your whole practice population.

Aims of personal development arising from the preliminary data-gathering exercise:

- To develop and implement an evidence-based referral protocol for primary and secondary infertility.
- To be able to explain the risks and benefits of common fertility treatments to patients who are anticipating receiving those treatments.

How you might integrate the 14 components of clinical governance into your personal development plan focusing on infertility practice

Establishing a learning culture: hold regular meetings on different aspects of infertility practice, including topics where the learning can be generalised to other conditions.

Managing resources and services: learn how to identify whether the computer system is being used to its best capacity in monitoring the care of those with infertility.

Establishing a research and development culture: introduce a system to update people's knowledge and skills as important new research is published – such a system might be generalised to medical conditions other than infertility.

Reliable and accurate data: keep good records so that you keep tabs on patients with infertility problems and minimise the chances of their becoming 'lost' in the system.

Evidence-based practice and policy: update your knowledge of the evidence with respect to infertility practice. Run a literature search or compare your referral and management practices with published guidelines.

Confidentiality: review your code of practice for confidentiality – for giving out results, responding to enquiries from a patient's family or estranged partner, or undertaking audits. Read up what is required, share your knowledge with others in your practice and apply it.

Health gain: better-quality management and more proactive care will result in health gains from fewer complications, etc.

Coherent team: everyone needs to know their roles and responsibilities in delivering care according to any practice protocol.

Audit and evaluation: follow up the management of infertility, search and audit care in a multiplicity of ways.

Meaningful involvement of patients and the public: provide health information requested by patients, e.g. in a newsletter written by both patients and staff. Use a patient focus group to discuss how you deliver patient care. Learn about methods of patient consultation and participation if you are unaware how to make patient and public involvement meaningful.

Health promotion: target health promotion with specific reminders on screen, or select specific groups for action, e.g. offer smoking cessation to anyone contemplating conception or who is already pregnant.

Risk management: reminders for action can be set on patients' computerised records.

Accountability and performance: you should be able to demonstrate that you are up-to-date in caring for those with infertility problems.

Core requirements: could you work out a better skill-mix in your practice team to provide more cost-effective or better co-ordinated care for those with infertility problems?

Action plan

Timetabled action: Start date . . .

By 3 months:
- Clarify the knowledge and skills you already have.
- Undertake a SWOT analysis of infertility management in the practice.
- Find out where training courses to match your needs can be accessed (in-practice, other practice(s), college or university, distance learning, other local or distant venue).

By 4 months:
- Carry out a selection of methods to record baseline performance, e.g. by undertaking a variety of the reflection exercises at the ends of the chapters.
- Sit in with hospital specialists at three infertility clinics.

By 6 months:
- Arrange the necessary training.
- Make a business plan for any associated equipment needs, e.g. a video camera if you are brushing up your communication skills.
- Arrange cover for yourself to provide protected time for learning.

- Rewrite the protocol for referring patients with primary infertility in discussion with consultants and other practices in the PCO.
- Negotiate changes in ways of working as necessary at practice meeting(s).

By 12 months:
- Implement the new system of procedures.
- Obtain feedback from other staff as to the impact of changes.
- Resolve any difficulties in the application of the new protocol.
- Identify any gaps in the provision of care and services to people with infertility.

Expected outcomes: better quality of care for patients, better access to care for patients, relevant inter-disciplinary shared information, less risk-taking by patients (depending on the exact project carried out).

How does your personal development plan tie in with other strategic plans?

The practice team wants someone to take a clinical lead on infertility matters; your keen interest ties in with the practice service development needs.

What resources will you require to execute your plan and from where do you hope to obtain them?

Your entitlement to reimbursement of course fees, etc., will depend on your contract and on the priority value that the practice or PCO puts on your development plan to meet their own needs.

Any additional equipment will have to be decided on the same basis.

How will you evaluate your learning plan?

Look at the methods you used to identify your learning needs – how does it all fit? Can you repeat a measure that you adopted to establish your learning needs to determine how much you have learnt or the extent to which your performance has improved?

How will you know when you have achieved your objectives?

You will be able to carry out the tasks you have set yourself, or will have implemented the changes specified in your objectives list.

How will you disseminate the learning from the plan to the rest of the practice team and patients and sustain your newfound knowledge or skills?

You might let everyone know in a practice newsletter. Let the staff know what has been achieved, or what is now available, at team meetings.

Pass on your skills to other people in the team as required. You could run an in-house training session to teach others in the practice team the new knowledge and skills you have mastered.

How will you handle new learning requirements as they crop up?

Keep a record of them as they arise to consider later or add them in if essential at this stage.

Check whether the topic you have chosen to learn is a priority and the way in which you plan to learn about it is appropriate.

> **Your topic:** *infertility matters*

How have you identified your learning need(s)?

(a) PCO requirement	☒	(e) Appraisal need	☐
(b) Practice business plan	☒	(f) New to post	☐
(c) Legal mandatory requirement	☐	(g) Individual decision	☐
(d) Job requirement	☒	(h) Patient feedback	☐
		(i) Other	☐

Have you discussed or planned your learning needs with anyone else?

Yes   ☒   No   ☐   If yes, who? *Other staff in the practice*

What are your learning need(s) and/or objective(s) in terms of:

Knowledge. What new information do you hope to gain to help you do this?
To learn what the risks and benefits of infertility investigations and treatments are.

Skills. What should you be able to do differently as a result of undertaking this learning in your development plan?

Undertake a larger proportion of infertility investigations in primary care before referring patients or couples to secondary care.

Behaviour/professional practice. How will this impact on the way you then do things?

I should be able to improve the quality of information I give to patients with infertility and reduce the time taken from presentation to treatment of infertility.

Details and date of desired development activity:

Within three months: attend updating sessions on infertility management and sit in on a few fertility clinic sessions with hospital specialist. Within six months: rewrite a referral protocol for people with primary infertility.

Details of any previous training and/or experience you have in this area/ dates:

Piecemeal self-instruction without structure or specific objectives.

What is your current performance in this area compared with the requirements of your job?

Need significant development in this area	X	Need some development in this area	☐
Satisfactory in this area	☐	Do well in this area	☐

What level of job relevance does this area have to your role and responsibilities?

Has no relevance to job	☐	Has some relevance	☐
Relevant to job	☐	Very relevant	X
Essential to job	☐		

Describe how the proposed education/training is relevant to your job:

Integral part of my work improving my expertise for patient groups with specific problems.

Do you need additional support in identifying a suitable development activity?

Yes ☒ No ☐

What do you need?

To know when and where relevant sessions of training are being held. Help in preparing to write a protocol.

Describe the differences or improvements for you, your practice, PCO and/or hospital trust as a result of undertaking this activity:

I will be able to evaluate the standards of care, monitor performance and assess progress towards targets set out in my personal development plan and the associated practice plan.

Assess the priority of your proposed educational/training activity:

Urgent ☐ High ☒ Medium ☐ Low ☐

Describe how the proposed activity will meet your learning needs rather than any other type of course or training on the topic:

The mix of learning from attendance at an updating course and clinic sessions should help me to identify what I don't know and meet my learning needs.

If you have a free choice would you want to learn this? *Yes*/No

If no, why not? (please circle all that apply):

It is a waste of time
I have already done it
It is not relevant to your work, career goals
Other

If yes, what reasons are most important to you (put in rank order):

To improve my performance	1
To increase my knowledge	2
To get promotion	
I am just interested in it	
To be better than my colleagues	
To do a more interesting job	
To be more confident	3

Record of your learning about infertility practice

You would add the date, length of time spent, etc., on each learning activity

	Activity 1: knowledge of best practice in infertility investigations	Activity 2: learning about infertility treatment techniques	Activity 3: learning about meaningful methods of patient and public involvement	Activity 4: learning to improve communication skills to patients
In-house formal learning	Hospital specialist attends in-house educational meeting	Hospital specialist attends in-house educational meeting	Member of patient organisation gives a brief talk to self and colleagues at practice meeting about importance of patient involvement	Protected time to use CD-ROM promoting communication skills; discussed with others operating CD-ROM
External courses	Attend updating course on infertility practice	Attend updating course on infertility practice		
Informal and personal	Sit in with nurse and consultant in three sessions at fertility clinic. Rewrite practice referral protocol and discuss contents with others in primary/secondary care	Sit in with nurse and consultant in three sessions at fertility clinic. Rewrite practice referral protocol and discuss contents with others in primary/secondary care	Read up on methods and apply previous experience of basic research methods	
Qualifications and/or experience gained	Experiences of others at the sessions; gain experience. Certificate of attendance at course	Certificate of attendance at course. Experience and practice	Written report of two patient-involvement exercises; one published in medical news-sheet	

Worked example 2. Personal development plan for a fertility nurse, GP or fertility specialist focusing on producing written information for patients

Why is the topic a priority?

(i) A personal or professional priority? Many aspects of infertility are complex and take time to understand, thus it is very helpful to have clear written information to give to patients following consultations.

(ii) A workplace priority? Explanation of infertility issues can take a considerable amount of time and if infertility questions arise unexpectedly during a busy clinic it may be difficult to allocate adequate time to answer these questions. By providing patients with written information this may more completely answer their immediate concerns and they may arrange a subsequent appointment for fuller discussion when they have read the information.

(iii) A district priority? If the written patient information is agreed between community and hospital, the patients will receive more integrated care and consistent messages from all healthcare professionals.

(iv) A national priority? Distributing patient information leaflets to colleagues will help everyone to make appropriate use of limited resources and help keep referrals appropriate. Including information on websites widens access to the information and allows direct reference to national societies, NHS and other appropriate websites.

Who will be included in your personal development plan?

You should consider inviting a senior colleague to act as a mentor, who could be a doctor or nurse.

How will you identify your learning needs?

Identify existing material prepared for patients by senior colleagues and national bodies. By reviewing your work in comparison to professional literature you may identify areas for improvement. Consider the clarity of your text: do you use unnecessary technical terms or fail to explain necessary complex terms? Is your text sufficiently concise while still including all-important key information?

If you are able to identify a mentor, then he/she may be able to give you a critical appraisal of your needs.

Identify the need in your workplace for a standard letter or a patient information sheet, such as general health advice for those trying for a baby, screening for viruses such as HIV and hepatitis prior to assisted conception treatment, or treatment options if a semen test reveals no sperm.

What are the learning needs of the practice or unit and how do they match your needs?

Depending on your role, you are likely to be involved with the production of variable amounts of patient-oriented information. However, communication with patients is vital for all health professionals and writing is a key form of communication.

Is there any patient or public input to your personal development plan?

Inviting patients to read and comment on your written patient information may provide useful feedback, but they are likely to be reluctant to criticise you. An alternative is to invite criticism from a lay person, possibly with experience in writing for the public.

Aims of your personal development plan arising from the preliminary data-gathering exercise:

Following the initial appraisal of your own writing skills you should identify areas for development. Once you have prioritised your practice's or unit's requirements for fertility patient information you will have established a worthwhile task to complete.

How you might integrate the 14 components of clinical governance into your personal development plan focusing on the topic of 'writing'

Establishing a learning culture: share the information with colleagues who have similar needs to yourself.

Managing resources and services: where standard information is presented to patients in individual letters, it may be possible to replace these letters with standard letters to save time, etc.

Establishing a research and development culture: encourage all colleagues to consider information needs for patients and produce literature where this is likely to be beneficial.

Reliable and accurate data: ensure the written information is correct by organising a peer review, and put in place a system to review the document at appropriate intervals to ensure that it does not become out of date.

Evidence-based practice and policy: information contained in your literature should be based on sound evidence. You may decide not to quote this in the patient document, but you should keep a separate record of these references so that you may refer to them later if necessary.

Confidentiality: ensure that your letters are sent to the correct patients at the correct address, especially if you are using standard letter templates.

Health gain: the better informed patients are about their healthcare, the greater their compliance and satisfaction with treatment should be.

Coherent team: all unit members need to be in agreement with any document that is produced by the unit.

Audit and evaluation: feedback from patients and audit of the use of an information sheet in practice will determine whether the information is achieving its goals.

Meaningful involvement of patients and the public: where patients criticise the literature that you provide, it should be reviewed with regard to changing the way that the information is presented.

Health promotion: target information where it may be useful. For instance, all women trying for a pregnancy may benefit from general health information covering smoking, alcohol, diet, folate supplement, etc.

Risk management: providing patients with written information may reduce the risk of them misunderstanding what you say.

Accountability and performance: need to review all patient information periodically.

Core requirements: encourage others to improve their writing skills in order to improve their communication with patients and outside bodies.

Action plan

Identify a mentor as soon as possible and discuss action plan with him/her.

By 3 months:
- Gather good examples of public information leaflets.
- Reflect on examples of your writing.
- Critically review examples of your writing with your mentor.
- Identify training course.
- Identify patient information leaflets that are required.
- Establish content for the above leaflets from reference material and colleagues.

By 4 months:
- Produce first drafts of your leaflets.

By 6 months:
- By this stage you should have been on a training course or about to start one.
- Undertake reflective exercise of your experience to date.
- Finalise first leaflet.
- Identify and start second patient information document.

By 12 months:
- Complete a training programme on writing skills.
- Use new skills.
- Identify where difficulties have arisen in the learning process and take steps to overcome them in partnership with your mentor.

Expected outcomes: improve personal ability in written communications, useful documents for patients, search of evidence upon which leaflets are based.

How does your personal development plan tie in with other strategic plans?

Improved communication with patients fits well with improving the overall quality of service, and standardised patient information may reduce costs and improve efficiency.

What additional resources will you require?

Reimbursement of course fees and protected time to produce documents. Funds to print information leaflets.

How will you evaluate your personal development plan?

Use your mentor to assess improvement and keep a reflective diary of your achievements.

How will you know when you have achieved your objectives?

Feedback from colleagues, including secretaries and patients, will help to establish if your patient information is helpful. An audit of the usage of the information will give objective measures of the usefulness or at least uptake of the written information.

How will you disseminate the learning from your plan to the rest of the practice team and patients and sustain your newfound knowledge or skills?

You may discuss your experience with others sharing your skills and perhaps encourage them to go on a writing course as well.

How will you handle new learning requirements as they crop up?

Once started, it is essential to continue writing to maintain your enthusiasm and skills. When you identify new learning requirements, such as writing for web pages, then you may repeat this exercise focusing on the new challenge of taking an appropriate course.

Record of your learning about producing written information for patients

You would add the date, length of time spent, etc., on each learning activity

	Activity 1: develop writing skills	Activity 2: identify topics for patients that your practice or unit would find useful	Activity 3: evaluate the success of your patient information document
In-house formal learning	Write an article aimed at patients and ask your mentor to critique this	Call a meeting of key staff saying that you wish to produce a patient information leaflet on infertility and ask your colleagues to suggest possible areas to cover	Discuss results of formal audit at team meeting and patients' views about current leaflets' perceived value
External courses	Attend writing course such as with the GP Writers Association (www.somw.org)	As you lack knowledge on the subject you wish to cover in the patient information, attend an appropriate course or lecture	
Informal and personal	Compare your written work with examples of best practice and read book on writing skills	Write the article based on valid published evidence and take advice from colleagues	Informal comment from your colleagues and mentor establishes the quality of your writing. Reflecting on your work at the end of the year in comparison to the start of the year will help you gauge your progress
Qualifications and/or experience gained	Certificate of attendance at course and theoretical knowledge about writing	Experience of writing for patients	Establish extent to which you have achieved your goals

Worked example 3. Personal development plan for a consultant fertility specialist focusing on the management of ovarian hyperstimulation syndrome

Why is the topic a priority?

(i) A personal or professional priority? Ovarian hyperstimulation syndrome (OHSS) is the cause of the most clinically significant short-term morbidity following gonadotrophin treatment. Thus, OHSS is an important consideration for anyone involved in gonadotrophin therapy.

(ii) A workplace priority? When a patient presents with OHSS it is important for all members of staff to be aware of the condition and the importance of appropriate assessment and management.

(iii) A district priority? Avoidance of OHSS reduces preventable ill health and costs of hospitalisation.

(iv) A national priority? Appropriate early management of OHSS reduces the likelihood of developing rare serious complications such as thrombo-embolic disease, with potential long-term consequences.

Who will be included in your personal development plan?

You might work on your own or involve:

- other doctors – hospital specialists
- nurses
- GPs
- patients.

What baseline information will you collect and how?

The incidence of OHSS in your practice and the number of cases admitted to hospital may be collected by reference to case notes. Depending on your local set-up and where patients are admitted to hospital, you may find that some hospital admissions are not recorded in your case notes. You may therefore need to seek the co-operation of other consultants to check on admissions to other local hospitals.

You might devise and circulate a questionnaire for patients who have suffered OHSS to see if they were satisfied with the information they received about their condition. You may introduce this prospectively and record the information following admission to hospital with OHSS.

It would be sensible to obtain general guidelines on the management of OHSS from appropriate sources such as professional journals or the advice provided by the Royal College of Obstetricians & Gynaecologists, with which to compare your practice.

How will you identify your learning needs?

By comparing your current practice with published guidelines you may identify areas that you wish to study in more depth. Reviewing your management of a few specific cases may further identify unclear areas, for which you may wish to refer to publications or colleagues for guidance.

Patients' views about OHSS may help to focus your attention on aspects that require particular explanation for patients. Areas to consider include whether the patients knew when to call for help and who to call, whether they appreciate the relationship between OHSS and pregnancy, and whether they felt that they had received adequate reassurance during the time they experienced OHSS.

What are the learning needs of the unit and how do they match your needs?

You may produce a standardised protocol for the management of OHSS for your unit. You may draft a comprehensive patient information sheet enabling all staff in your unit to provide consistent messages to patients.

Is there any patient or public input to your personal development plan?

Feedback of the experiences of patients who suffered OHSS may help considerably in your approach to managing OHSS and drafting a patient information leaflet.

Aims of your personal development plan arising from the preliminary data-gathering exercise:

It is important to focus your efforts where they will have most effect. At an early stage, identify the areas on which you need to take advice from guidelines and publications and draw up a list of the main questions to which patients would like to know the answers.

How might you integrate the 14 components of clinical governance into your personal development plan focusing on the topic of 'OHSS'?

Establishing a learning culture: invite all doctors and nurses to contribute to reviewing the evidence and devise the OHSS management guidelines and associated patient information leaflet.

Managing resources and services: decide which blood tests are necessary and establish appropriate criteria for hospital admission.

Establishing a research and development culture: where research has identified optimal management, include these in your guidelines.

Reliable and accurate data: collect information about cases of OHSS and check to ensure that guidelines have been followed in these cases.

Evidence-based practice and policy: management should be based on appropriate research or at least widely accepted practice endorsed by professional bodies, where possible.

Confidentiality: patient information about OHSS should be treated with strict confidentiality as with all clinical records. Audit data should be identified by a code rather than a patient name and should not contain any more information than is essential.

Health gain: appropriate early management may reduce the risks of later complications.

Coherent team: it is important for good management and patient confidence that nurses and doctors are consistent in what they say and do as individuals and as a team.

Audit and evaluation: it will become apparent whether current management is acceptable and whether this is room for improvement, by auditing the incidence and outcome of OHSS.

Meaningful involvement of patients and the public: responding to the feedback of patients may improve the care of patients with OHSS.

Health promotion: explaining the importance of early notification of symptoms will help to identify cases before serious problems arise.

Risk management: it is possible to target information and monitoring by identifying those patients at particular risk of developing OHSS.

Accountability and performance: it will be simpler to monitor professional management of individual cases if you have clear management guidelines and comprehensive medical records.

Core requirements: adherence to recommended best practice should make most efficient use of resources and help to ensure that patients receive optimal care.

Action plan

By 3 months:
Complete preliminary data gathering:
- Establish incidence of OHSS.
- Complete review of current literature.
- Obtain feedback from patients who have had OHSS.

By 4 months:
- Draft guidelines for the management of OHSS.
- Circulate to staff for comment.
- Attend updating course.

By 5 months:
- Draft patient OHSS information sheet for patients.
- Circulate to staff for comment.
- Ask patients to comment.
- Compare information sheet with a colleague's from another hospital.

By 6 months:
- Agree guidelines for management of OHSS with GPs at post-graduate education meeting.
- Agree patient OHSS information sheet for patients.

By 12 months:
- Audit to see if patients feel that the information has improved.
- Audit to see if guidelines for management of OHSS have been followed consistently.

How does your personal development plan tie in with other strategic plans?

OHSS is a clinical priority area and an important consideration in the overall service for ovarian stimulation with gonadotrophins.

What additional resources will you require to execute your plan and from where do you hope to obtain them?

It will be important to allocate protected administration time at intervals to ensure that the necessary activities have been completed.

You may be able to obtain the necessary information from your local medical library or an online resource such as the www.rcog.org.uk website or ReproMED website (www.ReproMED.net).

How will you evaluate your personal development plan?

You will be able to establish if you have followed the timetable and achieved the goals. A further audit after the introduction of the guidelines and information sheet will show whether you have improved outcomes.

How will you know when you have achieved your objectives?

Patient feedback and adherence to guidelines will show if you have achieved your goals.

How will you disseminate the learning from your plan to the rest of the team and patients and sustain your newfound knowledge or skills?

It may be useful to organise a team meeting when the management of OHSS is discussed in detail. This could start with the presentation of a few case studies of patients managed in your centre or unit followed by a general discussion.

It is important to review the literature on the management of OHSS constantly and modify your practice when new evidence emerges.

How will you handle new learning requirements as they crop up?

When major changes in management are suggested it may be necessary to consult with colleagues and professional bodies. Professional meetings may provide a good opportunity to learn about optimal management for OHSS in the light of latest evidence.

Record of your learning about OHSS

You would add the date, length of time spent, etc. on each learning activity

	Activity 1: understanding the causes and consequences of OHSS	Activity 2: establish what information patients need to know about OHSS	Activity 3: formulate evidence-based guidelines for management of OHSS
In-house formal learning		Analyse audit of patients' views on the information they wished to know about OHSS and discuss this at a formal meeting in your centre	Organise meeting to discuss the management guidelines you draft, based on review of evidence
External courses	Attend appropriate meeting organised by national body such as the British Fertility Society or Royal College of Obstetricians & Gynaecologists		
Informal and personal	Read appropriate literature from textbooks, journals and/or websites	Circulate draft patient information sheet for informal feedback ahead of formal meeting to discuss it	Circulate draft patient information sheet for informal feedback ahead of formal meeting to discuss it
Qualifications and/or experience gained	Certificate for attendance at course	Retain copy of summary of notes from audit in your personal portfolio	File a copy of the final management guidelines in your personal portfolio

Worked example 4. Personal development plan for an infertility nurse or infertility specialist focusing on ultrasound scanning

Why is the topic a priority?

(i) A personal or professional priority? Ultrasound examination of the pelvic structures is an essential investigation in routine fertility management. Thus, this is a valuable skill for anyone engaged in infertility management.

(ii) A workplace priority? If you are able to perform some of your own infertility scans rather than rely on others to do them, this will provide a more efficient and flexible service to patients.

(iii) A district priority? There may be considerable pressures on ultrasound services in your district and if the number of patients referred to these services can be reduced it may provide benefits even outside infertility services.

(iv) A national priority? Broadening the potential roles of healthcare professionals through training will lead to a more satisfied and flexible workforce, helping to retain staff and make more efficient use of existing staff.

Who will be included in your personal development plan?

They might include:

- a colleague who is experienced at ultrasound to act as a mentor
- members of the local ultrasound department team
- an outside educational body.

How will you identify your learning needs?

Review your experience of ultrasound. Consider the key skills you wish to develop, defining the area and level of scanning that you wish to achieve.

Identify a good text for baseline reading of the theory and practice of ultrasound. Compare aspects of your current practice.

Discuss your targets in consultation with a senior colleague who is appropriately experienced.

What are the learning needs of the centre or unit and how do they match your needs?

If you are already performing ultrasound scans in your routine practice, then the nature of the service your unit requires will help to define your targets. If your unit does not currently perform ultrasound scans then you should involve whoever performs your routine scans.

Is there any patient or public input to your personal development plan?

Your training will inevitably require you to scan patients, and it is important that you seek the permission from the patients who assist you in your training. Patient feedback should be valuable in relation to your technique and explanation of the investigations.

Aims of your personal development plan arising from the preliminary data-gathering exercise:

Once you have completed the basic data-gathering you should be able to define in what context you wish to develop your ultrasound skills and knowledge. You may decide to focus on vaginal ultrasound scans to monitor follicle growth during ovarian stimulation or you may include other areas such as ultrasound scans in early pregnancy and diagnostic assessment of the female pelvis. The target you set will determine the breadth and depth of training required.

How might you integrate the 14 components of clinical governance into your personal development plan focusing on the topic of 'ultrasound scanning'?

Establishing a learning culture: you may find that colleagues wish to develop, consolidate or extend their ultrasound skills. Thus, they may wish to join your training scheme.

Managing resources and services: you may change the pattern of integrated patient care if you are able to take on some of the ultrasound scans. If you learn more about the theory of how the ultrasound scanner works, you may be able to resolve some technical problems rather than call on the support technician.

Establishing a research and development culture: you may realise opportunities for research once you have developed your ultrasound skills.

Reliable and accurate data: it is essential that your ultrasound scans are reliable and accurate, thus it will be important to check your results against those of a more experienced practitioner.

Evidence-based practice and policy: you need to base your ultrasound practice on evidence establishing appropriate guidelines that others in your unit may also follow.

Confidentiality: vaginal ultrasonography is a very intimate examination, thus it is particularly important to respect a patient's confidentiality and privacy.

Health gain: if you improve the availability and standard of ultrasound scans in your practice, this will improve the quality of patient care.

Coherent team: if focused ultrasound skills are developed as part of a coherent strategy of care, this may improve the teamworking, as well as helping the infertile couple.

Audit and evaluation: it is essential to evaluate and audit practice, particularly during training. But even later in your career, it is sensible to compare results and techniques of different team members to ensure consistency.

Meaningful involvement of patients and the public: patients may provide useful information to ensure that you are not causing them unnecessary discomfort.

Health promotion: there is an opportunity to talk to patients more generally while performing an ultrasound scan. For instance, you could check that they are taking folic acid supplements to reduce the risk of neural tube defects.

Risk management: inaccurate ultrasound scans can lead to incorrect diagnosis or management, thus reliability is important. If you are unsure, acknowledge this and ask for help.

Accountability and performance: you are accountable for your practice, thus you should be able to provide evidence of training and ongoing evaluation.

Core requirements: ultrasonography is essential in modern infertility practice and development of skills in this area should certainly be encouraged.

Action plan

Identify a mentor as soon as possible and discuss your action plan with him/her.

By 3 months:
- Define personal targets.
- Familiarise yourself with the basic controls of an ultrasound machine.
- Draft a training plan with your mentor.
- Identify appropriate training course and book.

By 6 months:
- Undertake ultrasound scans under supervision including keeping records in training diary.
- Undertake a reflective exercise on your experience.
- Review your training diary with your mentor and identify where difficulties have arisen in the learning process.
- Start an audit on the number of scans you do and the outcomes.
- Arrange training course.

By 12 months:
- Complete the training course
- Complete the audit of your ultrasound scans, present the results to your mentor and review your performance.

Expected outcomes: improved ultrasound technique, better understanding of ultrasonography, improved care for patients.

How does your personal development plan tie in with other strategic plans?

Improving your ultrasound skills may enable you to develop your role in ovulation induction treatment for patients. This would require separate theoretical and practical training.

What additional resources will you require?

You may require reimbursement of course fees, more time with patients to gain experience with ultrasound scans and protected time for study.

How will you evaluate your personal development plan?

You may find it best to reflect on your own practice using a training diary and then discuss it with your mentor.

How will you know when you have achieved your objectives?

You should feel confident in performing the scans unaided and have satisfied the pre-agreed criteria set with your mentor.

How will you disseminate the learning from your plan to the rest of the team and patients and sustain your newfound knowledge or skills?

You may share your skills with other team members at a specially convened educational meeting. You will incorporate ultrasound scans into your routine practice, perhaps allocating specific scanning sessions.

How will you handle new learning requirements as they crop up?

Once started, it is essential to continue to use your ultrasound skills to maintain proficiency. When you identify new learning requirements, such as undertaking ultrasound scans for a further clinical indication, then you may repeat this exercise, focusing on the new challenge after first attending an appropriate course.

Record of your learning on ultrasound scanning

You would add the date, length of time spent, etc., on each learning activity

	Activity 1: theoretical knowledge of ultrasound scanning	*Activity 2: practical experience in ultrasound scanning*	*Activity 3: interpretation of ultrasound scans*
In-house formal learning	Ultrasonographer or other expert provides formal presentation on ultrasound scanning in your unit	Observe a series of ultrasound scans by mentor/experienced colleague. Perform a series of ultrasound scans under the direct supervision of your mentor	If your main interest is in follicular scanning for ovulation induction, you would benefit from attending a lecture on this
External courses	Attend formal ultrasound scanning course	Attend as observer at ultrasound sessions in local ultrasound department	A formal course on ovulation induction helps to clarify your management of ultrasound scans
Informal and personal	Read articles about the theory and practice of ultrasonography	Keep a diary of the ultrasounds you have performed. Over time, reflect on progress in your confidence, ease of performing scans and quality of pictures, with mentor	Reading appropriate articles will help to consolidate your knowledge
Qualifications and/or experience gained	Certificate of attendance at course and theoretical knowledge	Essential practical experience of performing ultrasound scans	Understanding how to interpret ultrasound scans helps to focus your attention appropriately when you are performing scans

APPENDIX 1

Organisations

British Infertility Counselling Association

69 Division Street, Sheffield S1 4GE
Tel: 01342 843880; fax: 01663 765285
www.bica.net
info@bica.net

Centre for Reproductive Medicine, Bristol

University of Bristol, 4 Priory Road, Clifton, Bristol BS8 1TY
Tel: 0117 902 1100; fax: 0117 902 1101
www.ReproMED.co.uk

CHILD

Charter House, St Leonards Road, Bexhill on Sea, East Sussex TN40 1JA
Tel: 01424 732361; fax: 01424 731858
www.child.org.uk/
office@child.org.uk

Human Fertilisation and Embryology Authority

Paxton House, 30 Artillery Lane, London E1 7LS
Tel: 020 7377 5077; fax: 020 7377 1871
www.hfea.gov.uk/
admin@hfea.gov.uk

Issue (The National Fertility Association) (DI Network has been incorporated into Issue)

114 Lichfield Street, Walsall WS1 1SZ
Tel: 01922 722888; fax: 01922 640070
www.issue.co.uk
info@issue.co.uk

Miscarriage Association

c/o Clayton Hospital, Northgate, Wakefield, West Yorkshire WF1 3JS
Tel: 01924 200799; fax: 01924 298834
www.miscarriageassociation.org.uk
info@miscarriageassociation.org.uk

Multiple Births Foundation

Level 4, Hammersmith House, Queen Charlotte's & Chelsea Hospital,
Du Cane Road, London W12 0HS
Tel: 020 8383 3519; fax: 020 8383 0341
www.multiplebirths.org.uk
info@multiplebirths.org.uk

National Infertility Awareness Campaign

PO Box 2106, London W1A 3DZ
Tel: 020 7439 3067; fax: 020 7437 0553
www.repromed.co.uk/NIAC/

RELATE

Herbert Gray College, Little Church Street, Rugby, Warwickshire
CV21 3AP
Tel: 01788 573241
www.relate.org.uk/
enquiries@relate.org.uk

Royal College of Obstetricians and Gynaecologists

27 Sussex Place, Regent's Park, London NW1 4RG
Tel: 020 7772 6200
www.rcog.org.uk

APPENDIX 2

Books/booklets

Brian K (1998) *In Pursuit of Parenthood*. Bloomsbury, London.

British Medical Association (1996) *Considering Surrogacy?* BMA, London.

Cahill D and Wardle P (2000) *Understanding Infertility*. Family Doctor Publications, Poole.

Family Planning Association (1998) *Infertility Tests and Treatment*. fpa, PO Box 1078, East Oxford OD, Oxfordshire OX4 5JE.

Furse A (1997) *Infertility Companion: a user's guide to tests, technologies and therapies*. Thorsons, London.

Hammer Burns L and Covington S (1998) *Infertility Counselling. A comprehensive handbook for clinicians*. Parthenon, London.

Human Fertilisation and Embryology Authority:

   (i) The Patients' Guide to Infertility and IVF (2002) (free from the HFEA)

   (ii) Code of Practice 2001

   (iii) Annual Report 2001

   (iv) Videos: *In vitro* fertilisation and donor insemination

   (v) Website: www.hfea.gov.uk

Johnson M and Everitt BJ (1995) *Essential Reproduction*. Blackwell Science, Oxford.

Mack S and Tucker J (1996) *Fertility Counselling*. Baillière Tindall, London.

Royal College of Obstetricians and Gynaecologists (1998) *The initial investigation and management of the infertile couple. Evidence-based clinical guidelines. No. 2*. Royal College of Obstetricians and Gynaecologists, London.

Royal College of Obstetricians and Gynaecologists (1998) *The management of infertility in secondary care. Evidence-based clinical guidelines. No. 3*. Royal College of Obstetricians and Gynaecologists, London.

Tan SL and Jacobs HS (1991) *Infertility: your questions answered*. McGraw-Hill, London.

Winston, R (1994) *Infertility: a sympathetic approach*. Vermilion, London.

Glossary

Artificial insemination (AI): Artificial introduction of sperm into the reproductive tract. Sperm may be from the husband (AIH) or from a donor (DI). The sperm may be deposited in the cervical os (ICI) or directly into the uterus (IUI).

Assisted hatching (AH, AZH): Thinning of the shell surrounding the embryo (zona pellucida) prior to transferring the embryo into the uterus, which may improve pregnancy rates for certain patients having IVF.

Assisted reproductive technology (ART): A general term covering procedures employed to bring about conception without sexual intercourse, including IUI, IVF, GIFT and ZIFT.

Blastocyst transfer: Allowing *in vitro* fertilised embryos to reach blastocyst stage (usually takes five days) before transferring the embryos into the uterus.

Consent: A person donating his or her genetic material or a patient undergoing infertility treatment must consent to the procedure in the same way as for any other medical treatment. The consent must be valid and informed. The storage and use of genetic material requires written effective consent.

Controlled ovarian hyperstimulation (COH): Using gonadotrophin stimulation to stimulate the growth of multiple follicles, usually to increase the number of oocytes available for IVF. Also called super-ovulation.

Cryopreservation of gametes and embryos: Freezing and then storing sperm, embryos and, more recently, unfertilised eggs for later treatment.

Direct intra-peritoneal insemination (DIPI, IPI): Injection of sperm into the peritoneal cavity. A form of artificial insemination that may be used when there is no access to the cervix, for instance with certain congenital abnormalities.

Donor insemination (DI): Artificial insemination with donor sperm.

Egg donation: The act of donating eggs to someone else for use in attempting pregnancy through IVF.

Egg retrieval: A procedure used to obtain eggs from ovarian follicles for use in several ARTs, including IVF and GIFT. The procedure may be performed during laparoscopy but is usually carried out using a needle guided by ultrasound to locate the follicle in the ovary.

Electroejaculation: A controlled electric stimulation to induce ejaculation of semen in a man, who is unable to ejaculate naturally, usually due to damage to the nerves that control ejaculation.

Embryo: A fertilised egg up to eight weeks of development.

Embryo transfer (ET): Placing an egg fertilised outside the womb into a woman's uterus (transcervical embryo transfer) or fallopian tube (tubal embryo transfer).

Fetus: The term used for an embryo after the eighth week of development until birth.

Follicle: A small sac in the ovary in which the egg develops.

Frozen embryo transfer (FET): A procedure where frozen (cryopreserved) embryos are thawed and then placed into the uterus, either at the appropriate time of a natural menstrual cycle or following preparation of the uterus with hormone replacement therapy.

Gamete: A reproductive cell such as an ovum or a spermatozoon which has a haploid set of chromosomes and which is able to take part in fertilisation with another of the opposite sex to form a zygote.

Gamete intrafallopian transfer (GIFT): After egg retrieval the eggs are mixed with sperm and then immediately injected into the woman's fallopian tubes under laparoscopic guidance so that fertilisation occurs *in vivo*.

Hysteroscopic surgery: A procedure to examine intrauterine abnormalities by inserting a fibre-optic device through the cervix. Minor surgical procedures can be executed during the procedure, such as removal of adhesions or polyps.

Intracervical insemination (ICI): Artificial insemination where the sperm is deposited into the cervical canal.

Intracytoplasmic sperm injection (ICSI): A procedure in which a single sperm is injected into the egg to enable fertilisation with very low sperm counts or other sperm problems, such as non-motile sperm.

Intrauterine insemination (IUI): Prepared sperm are inserted directly into the uterus, bypassing cervical mucus thus depositing the sperm more closely to the fallopian tubes, where fertilisation occurs. Used to bypass hostile cervical mucus and in an attempt to overcome sperm count and motility problems. This may be combined with superovulation, although this risks multiple pregnancy.

In vitro fertilisation (IVF): The combining of the genetic material carried by sperm and egg to create an embryo, usually in a small plastic dish, although literally, *in vitro* means 'in glass'.

Laparoscopic surgery: Surgical procedures performed using instruments introduced through small incisions in the abdomen under vision through a fibre-optic device (laparoscope) usually inserted just below the umbilicus.

Licensed treatment: Any fertilisation treatment which involves the use of donated eggs or sperm (e.g. donor insemination) or where embryos are created outside of the body (e.g. *in vitro* fertilisation).

Live birth rate: The number of live births achieved with 100 treatment cycles.

Microsurgical epididymal sperm aspiration (MESA): Using micro-surgery to remove sperm from the epididymis, which is a collection of tubules storing sperm at the head of the testis.

Myomectomy: Removal of a fibroid from the uterus.

Ovarian hyperstimulation syndrome (OHSS): An adverse reaction that occurs in a small percentage of women receiving ovarian stimulating drugs. Symptoms include abdominal discomfort and swelling, nausea and vomiting, and in extreme cases, ascites, plural effusion and venous thrombosis.

Ovulation induction therapy: Fertility treatments, ovulate including clomiphene and gonadotrophins, designed to help infertile women.

Partial zona dissection (PZD): An inefficient predecessor to ICSI in which the zona pellucida, or shell, surrounding a woman's egg is opened, using either chemical dissolution or mechanical methods with a microneedle, to facilitate access for sperm to the egg.

Percutaneous epididymal sperm aspiration (PESA): A small needle is passed through the skin directly into the head of the epididymis and fluid is aspirated.

Personal development plan (PDP): *See* Chapter 10.

Pre-implantation diagnosis (PGD): A technique to detect inherited genetic disorders in embryos *in vitro* before transfer to the uterus; the procedure entails removing one or more cells from an embryo for genetic analysis, usually at about two to three days after fertilisation when the embryo consists of 8–16 cells.

Salpingolysis: Division of fallopian tube adhesions, usually to improve fertility.

Spermatid: An immature precursor of spermatozoa.

Subzonal insertion (SUZI): An inefficient predecessor to ICSI where the zona pellucida is punctured and sperm inserted into the area between the zona and the egg.

Superovulation: Using fertility medications to stimulate the growth of multiple follicles for ovulation. Also known as controlled ovarian hyperstimulation (COH).

Surgical sperm retrieval (SSR): A general term covering techniques to obtain sperm from men whose ejaculate may contain no sperm, including PESA, MESA, TESE and TESA. Sperm collected may be used immediately for ICSI or cryopreserved for later treatment.

Surrogacy: A woman is inseminated or receives embryos produced by an IVF procedure using the intended mother's eggs, and carries to term a baby that will be adopted and raised by another couple. The term is usually used for a woman who is the biological mother of the baby she is carrying, while a gestational host carries a fetus that is not genetically hers.

Testicular sperm aspiration (TESA): A needle biopsy of the testicle used to obtain small amounts of sperm. A small incision is made in the scrotal skin and a spring-loaded needle is fired through the testicle.

Testicular sperm extraction (TESE): An open biopsy where a small piece of testicular tissue is removed through a skin incision. The tissue is placed in culture media and separated into tiny pieces. Sperm are released from within the seminiferous tubules where they are produced, and are then extracted from the surrounding testicular tissue.

Tubal embryo transfer (TET): The placement of an embryo inside the fallopian tube after *in vitro* fertilisation. The process is meant to mimic the natural process of a fertilised embryo travelling down the tube and implanting in the uterus.

Tubocornual anastomosis: Surgery performed to remove a blocked portion of the fallopian tube and to reconnect the tube to the uterus. Tubouterine implantation may also be performed to remove fallopian tube blockage near the uterus and reimplant the tube in the uterus.

Tuboplasty: Surgery on the fallopian tubes to correct abnormalities which may lead to blockage or otherwise cause infertility.

Tubotubal anastomosis: Surgery performed to remove a defective portion of the fallopian tube and reconnect the two ends, such as with reversal of female sterilisation.

Vasectomy reversal: Surgical reanastomosis of the vas following previous vasectomy aiming to restore fertility.

Vibroejaculation: A vibrator is used to induce ejaculation of semen in a man who is unable to ejaculate naturally. This is simpler but less effective than electroejaculation.

Zygote intrafallopian transfer (ZIFT): A technique in which eggs are removed from a woman's ovaries, fertilised with the man's sperm in a laboratory dish, and the resulting zygotes (day 1 fertilised eggs) are transferred into a woman's fallopian tubes by laparoscopy.

To view the extended glossary please visit www.ReproMED.org.uk/book/.

Index